RA

Science and Technol

BUILDING BETTER HOMES

Government Strategies for Promoting Innovation in Housing

Scott Hassell

Anny Wong

Ari Houser

Debra Knopman

Mark Bernstein

Prepared for the
U.S. Department of Housing and Urban Development (HUD)
Office of Policy Development and Research and
the Partnership for Advancing Technology in Housing (PATH)

The research described in this report was conducted by RAND's Science and Technology Policy Institute for the U.S. Department of Housing and Urban Development (HUD) Office of Policy Development and Research and the Partnership for Advancing Technology in Housing (PATH), under contract number ENG-9812731.

Library of Congress Cataloging-in-Publication Data

Building better homes : government strategies for promoting innovation in housing / Scott Hassell ... [et al.].
    p. cm.
    "MR-1658."
    Includes bibliographical references and index.
    ISBN 0-8330-3332-8 (pbk.)
    1. Housing policy—United States. I. Hassell, Scott, 1974–.

HD7293.B825 2003
333.33'8'0973—dc21

2002155749

RAND is a nonprofit institution that helps improve policy and decisionmaking through research and analysis. RAND® is a registered trademark. RAND's publications do not necessarily reflect the opinions or policies of its research sponsors.

Published 2003 by RAND
1700 Main Street, P.O. Box 2138, Santa Monica, CA 90407-2138
1200 South Hayes Street, Arlington, VA 22202-5050
201 North Craig Street, Suite 202, Pittsburgh, PA 15213-1516
RAND URL: http://www.rand.org/
To order RAND documents or to obtain additional information, contact Distribution Services: Telephone: (310) 451-7002; Fax: (310) 451-6915; Email: order@rand.org

This study was prepared in response to a request from the U.S. Department of Housing and Urban Development (HUD) Office of Policy Development and Research and the Partnership for Advancing Technology in Housing (PATH).

This report describes the importance of innovation in the U.S. housing industry, discusses the factors affecting such innovation, summarizes past efforts by the federal government to promote innovation, and suggests strategies that the federal government should consider to increase the rate of innovation in housing. The report was prepared for a broad audience including federal, state, and local government officials, participants in the homebuilding process, and those interested in better promotion and acceleration of innovation in housing.

Originally created by Congress in 1991 as the Critical Technologies Institute and renamed in 1998, the Science and Technology Policy Institute is a federally funded research and development center sponsored by the National Science Foundation and managed by RAND. The institute's mission is to help improve public policy by conducting objective, independent research and analysis on policy issues that involve science and technology. To this end, the institute

- supports the Office of Science and Technology Policy and other Executive Branch agencies, offices, and councils

- helps science and technology decisionmakers understand the likely consequences of their decisions and choose among alternative policies

- helps improve understanding in both the public and private sectors of the ways in which science and technology can better serve national objectives. In carrying out its mission, the institute consults broadly with representatives from private industry, institutions of higher education, and other nonprofit institutions.

Inquiries regarding the Science and Technology Policy Institute may be directed to the addresses below.

Helga Rippen
Director
Science and Technology Policy Institute

Science and Technology Policy Institute	
RAND	Tel: (703) 413-1100, ext. 5574
1200 South Hayes Street	Web: http://www.rand.org/scitech/stpi
Arlington, VA 22202-5050	Email: stpi@rand.org

CONTENTS

FIGURES

TABLES

This report examines the structure, characteristics, and motivations of major participants in the housing industry to explore how innovation might be improved or accelerated within the industry as it currently exists. This approach recognizes that the housing industry is large and complex and changing any part would be difficult and changing the whole practically impossible. In this context, the report identifies options and strategies for the federal government to consider as it continues to further advance innovation in housing to make homes more affordable, durable, and safe for their occupants and builders, and to provide other benefits to society.

INNOVATION IS IMPORTANT TO THE U.S. HOUSING INDUSTRY

There have been many significant housing innovations in the last 100 years. Notable examples include the introduction of electricity and air conditioning, standardized building products such as 2x4 plywood boards, and factory-made components including roof trusses and kitchen cabinets.

These innovations have changed what homes are made of, how they are built, how they perform, who can afford them, and how well they serve their occupants. As a result of these improvements—referred to as *innovations* in this report—housing has improved significantly for most people and for the nation's quality of life in general.

Innovation in housing has important economic ramifications. The U.S. housing industry represents nearly 20 percent of the nation's gross domestic product. It includes millions of people who design, build, finance, furnish, and maintain the nation's housing stock. It also represents the value of more than 115 million homes currently in stock and the nearly two million new units built each year.[1] In short, housing is the largest component of the nation's physical wealth. Perhaps even more important, homes are the largest expenditure in most household budgets and a home is usually the most valuable asset a family owns.

The assertion that the rate of innovation in housing has slowed or is slow compared to that in other industries is not uncommon among industry and other entities. However, there is no consensus on this claim, and a lack of data makes it difficult and perhaps impossible to verify.

Regardless of whether the rate of innovation in housing has slowed or is slower than that in other industries, innovation contributes positively to increase productivity and provide other benefits to all who are involved in housing. This would include a broad range of housing industry participants from homebuilders to manufacturers, insurers, regulators, homeowners, and others.

ACCELERATING INNOVATION IN THE CURRENT INDUSTRY CONTEXT

Concern for innovation in housing has prompted industry, government, and researchers to find ways to accelerate it in the housing industry. Driven by an implicit (and sometimes explicit) assumption that innovation is a natural occurrence, held back only by certain obstacles, many workshops, roundtables, surveys, research, and other efforts have tried to identify barriers to innovation and ways to overcome them. These efforts often end up pointing to certain structures and characteristics of the industry as barriers and recommending a range of actions, including government intervention and industry reform, to eliminate them and make way for innovation.

---

[1] "Homes" in this study include both single- and multifamily housing units. Hence, homes or housing units include houses, apartment buildings, condominiums, townhouses, and manufactured homes among others.

That such prescriptions have not led to a higher rate of innovation or more innovations in the housing industry is not entirely surprising. Indeed, many industry features can affect innovation, including the following:

- Its highly competitive nature may deter industry participants from adopting innovations because they want to minimize risks.

- The boom-bust cycles lead to low investment in employees and training to prepare them for innovation.

- Dominance of the housing industry by small and medium-size homebuilders means that few have the resources to innovate.

- The fragmented nature of the industry slows information sharing and innovation acceptance.

- Construction is done in the open and the process involves a variety of independent actors so it is difficult for innovators to protect innovations (as intellectual properties) and exploit their competitive advantages long before others copy and use them.

However, designating these and other industry characteristics as barriers for removal may not be the best way to promote innovation, because the housing industry is large and complex, involving many public and private entities. The interests, roles, and capacities of each participant and the relationships they share have shaped the housing industry into what it is today and changing certain industry structures and characteristics means asking participants to change as well. For such a large and complex industry, any change in parts would be difficult and any change in its entirety would be practically impossible.

For this reason, this study takes a different approach to exploring how innovation might be accelerated in the housing industry. Instead of trying to identify barriers and asking the industry to change itself (or asking the government to change it), this study seeks to identify options to accelerate innovation within the housing industry as it currently exists. It begins by critically examining the concept of innovation and how it might be better understood within the context of the housing industry. What results is a departure from the linear model of innovation that assumes logical and unidirectional movement from research to development, demonstration, and deployment to one that recognizes much greater interactive dynamics in the innovation process. Research, in this model, is a base for knowledge, which contributes to invention, development, demonstration, and deployment. Moreover, all these activities or stages in the innovation process are affected by market forces. Therefore, whether an innovation emerges and goes through the innovation process and results in widespread adoption is not an automatic or natural progression (see Figure S.1).

To better explore how this model to understanding innovation might find application in the housing industry, this study then examines the structure and characteristics of the housing industry and the motivations that might drive industry participants to accept or reject innovation.

RAND MR1658-S.1

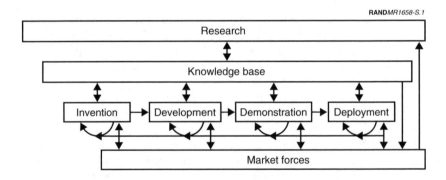

Figure S.1—Innovation as the Invention, Development, Demonstration, and Deployment Process

PROPOSALS FOR FEDERAL GOVERNMENT ACTION

Since the federal government has an interest in increasing innovation in housing, specific options for federal action are put forth. These proposals are made with full appreciation of the federal government's involvement in innovation in housing over the past 30 years. Investment in research for this study indicates a commitment to increasing innovation in housing and willingness to experiment with new ideas and approaches as the federal government works with industry and other interested participants.

These proposals are divided into four categories:

- enhance research activities,

- strengthen the knowledge base,

- support product development, and

- improve market linkages.

Under each category are a number of strategies for federal consideration (see Table S.1). These strategies are not exhaustive or exclusive. They are meant to illustrate actions for consideration. It was beyond the scope of this study to take the next step—to examine cost-effectiveness or how one strategy might work with another.

These potential strategies could enable the federal government to advance innovation by better leveraging what it is already doing and

Table S.1

Strategies for Promoting Innovation in Housing

Enhance Research Activities
Sustain support for research

Strengthen the Knowledge Base
Support networking across horizontal and vertical boundaries
Coordinate government efforts
Search for and disseminate information on relevant federal R&D
Support education and training

Support Product Development
Support exploratory and applied research for technology transfer
Modify the research and experiment tax credit for small firms
Support development and demonstration
Explain the regulatory process to innovators
Provide technical and standard development support
Use public procurement

Improve Market Linkages
Help identify market trends and opportunities
Support product performance monitoring and evaluation
Reward important innovations with valuable recognition
Create linkages between markets
Create financial incentives for end users

what currently exists in the housing industry. In short, these strategies would focus resources on doing what is possible and practical to achieve measurable success.

ACKNOWLEDGMENTS

The authors would like to thank many individuals in the private sector, government, and academia who shared their time and insights during the past three years. Their assistance helped us to better understand the housing industry and its many participants, perspectives, and challenges. In particular, we would like to thank Carlos E. Martin and David Engel of the U.S. Department of Housing and Urban Development; John Talbott of the U.S. Department of Energy; Andy Fowell, previously of the National Institute of Standards and Technology; David Dacquisto, Ross Heitzmann, and Larry Zarker; and David Conover of the National Evaluation Service.

We would also like to thank those who reviewed and critiqued this report, in particular, William Butz and David Adamson of RAND and Ronald Wakefield of Virginia Polytechnic Institute and State University. Finally, we thank Heather Roy for her help in preparing the manuscript.

AHTP	Advanced Housing Technology Program
ATP	Advanced Technology Program
CRADA	Cooperative Research and Development Agreement
DOC	U.S. Department of Commerce
DOE	U.S. Department of Energy
EEM	Energy Efficiency Mortgage
EIFS	External Insulation Finishing Systems
EPA	Environmental Protection Agency
GDP	Gross domestic product
HUD	U.S. Department of Housing and Urban Development
HVAC	Heating, ventilating, and air-conditioning
IBHS	Institute for Business and Home Safety
ICC	International Code Council
ICF	Insulating concrete forms
ID3	Invention, development, demonstration, and deployment
IOF	Industries of the Future
IT	Information technology
MEP	Manufacturing Extension Program
NAHB	National Association of Home Builders
NIST	National Institute of Standards and Technology

NSF	National Science Foundation
NSTC	The National Science and Technology Council
PAIR	Partnership for the Advancement of Infrastructure and Its Renewal
PATH	Partnership for Advancing Technology in Housing
PCAST	President's Council of Advisors on Science and Technology
R&D	Research and Development
RDDD or RD3	Research, development, demonstration, and deployment
SBIR	Small Business Innovation Research

Chapter One

INNOVATION IN HOUSING

Housing in the United States comes in varied forms depending on land, climate, and available resources. Over time, changes in design, materials, building techniques, financing, and planning have changed what homes are made of, how they are built, what we can do in them, and who can afford them. As a result of these changes—referred to as *innovations* in this report—the quality and nature of housing have improved significantly, although not evenly for all inhabitants in all places and times.

The true value of innovation is that it is a means to an end. For example, innovations in housing provide homeowners with more for less; enable homebuilders to build more-desirable homes at lower cost; and help governments address major challenges such as making homes more affordable, improving energy efficiency, and reducing susceptibility to natural disasters.

As will be discussed in this report, the housing industry is often described as having many characteristics that challenge the development and deployment of innovations. If this description is true, then a poorly functioning housing innovation system will undoubtedly deprive homeowners, homebuilders, and society of the benefits that innovation can provide. These concerns have led to recommendations that the federal government support innovation in housing.

The Congress and federal agencies have, in fact, been involved in innovation in housing for more than three decades through investment in research and programmatic activities. Federal efforts to promote innovation have also modified strategies and tactics over time to better work with industry, and this evolution continues today.

This study examines the rationale and strategies available to the federal government for promoting and accelerating innovation in housing.[1] It approaches this task by exploring how innovation might be improved or accelerated in the housing industry as it currently exists. This approach is chosen because the authors consider it more pragmatic to solving problems than approaches that emphasize barrier identification and analysis and look for solutions that call for restructuring the industry. The housing industry is so large and complex that changing any part would be difficult and changing the whole is practically impossible. This might explain why there has been little apparent success in implementing proposals from such studies.

This study begins by examining how the concept of innovation might be understood within the context of the U.S. housing industry. Next, housing industry structure and characteristics are described to better understand how they affect motives for innovation among major industry participants and to better understand the setting in which innovation occurs. Following this, past and current federal efforts to promote innovation in housing are studied to set the stage for the introduction of a conceptual framework and list of recommendations for federal consideration in selecting strategies to advance innovation in housing.

THE BENEFITS OF INNOVATION IN HOUSING

The benefits of innovation to homeowners have been significant. The professionalization of the homebuilding process, the installation of indoor plumbing, the introduction of electricity, and the development and implementation of building codes, among other innovations, have led to homes that provide a safe, secure, and comfortable environment; protect life and property; and fulfill many of our daily needs.

Innovation has also brought significant benefits to homebuilders. Standardized building products such as 2x4s, roof trusses, and

---

[1]This report focuses on actions that the federal government can take to promote housing innovation. Although the authors believe that the report will be useful to state and local governments by providing information that could help them formulate their own strategies for promoting innovation, this is not the focus of this report.

factory-made kitchen cabinets have enabled builders to improve housing quality while lowering costs. In addition, by using innovative materials and techniques including energy-efficient design and construction, "green" building materials, and senior-friendly housing design, builders have been able to differentiate their homes from those of their competitors thereby creating market niches for their services.

The benefits of innovation also accrue to society. Most obviously, since everyone owns, rents, or seeks some form of housing, the entire nation stands to benefit from innovations that improve neighborhoods, towns, quality of life, the economy, and the environment. For example, innovation has helped keep housing affordable and the economy growing; worker productivity increased nearly 2 percent a year on average between 1972 and 2000.[2] Financing innovations have also benefited society by boosting homeownership to an all-time high of 68 percent of the U.S. population in 2001.[3] In addition, energy-efficiency innovations reduced residential energy consumption 27 percent between 1978 and 1997.[4] Finally, regulatory innovations such as performance-based building codes[5] and Internet-based permit services are helping to protect life and property at lower cost and with greater flexibility.

As these examples demonstrate, innovation affects national productivity and economic growth, homeownership rates and related socioeconomic issues,[6] energy consumption, a broad range of environmental issues (e.g., air pollution, water scarcity, and solid waste), as well as society's ability to protect life and property.

------

[2]Data on fixed residential investment and production workers are from U.S. Department of Commerce (2002).

[3]U.S. Census Bureau, Table 5 (2002a).

[4]Energy Information Administration (2002).

[5]Performance-based building codes state what a material or method must achieve rather than what must be done and how to do it. This makes performance-based building codes more versatile and accommodating to both conventional and innovative technologies.

[6]The affordability of housing and homeownership rates in particular are often associated with building stronger communities, strengthening families, and creating stability for children. For a discussion, see Rohe et al. (2000).

CHALLENGES TO INNOVATION IN THE HOUSING INDUSTRY

Despite the many innovations that occurred over the last century, the conventional wisdom is that innovation is slower in housing than in other industries. Two measures commonly used to support this argument are the industry's small investments in research and development (R&D) and the long adoption/diffusion times for new technologies.[7] Other challenges to innovation frequently cited by the industry include the industry's complex and fragmented structure; its highly competitive and risky nature; the difficulty in accessing and sharing information; local variation in regulatory requirements and their implementation; the low levels of skill, training, and investment throughout much of the industry and its workforce; and the difficulty of protecting innovations and appropriating their financial returns.

Although studies disagree on the precise state of innovation in housing and on the relative importance of the contributing factors, it is more important to recognize that more innovation would be beneficial regardless of how much is occurring. However, increasing innovation is difficult for individual homeowners, homebuilders, and even significant portions of the industry, since many of the challenges to innovation are industrywide. For this reason, studies have long recommended that the federal government support housing-related R&D as well as the larger housing innovation system.

FEDERAL GOVERNMENT SUPPORT OF HOUSING INNOVATION

The legislative and executive branches of the federal government have long recognized the challenges facing innovation in housing and have supported efforts to increase innovation. These efforts have evolved over time, but one of the earliest and clearest congressional charges was in the Housing and Urban Development Act of 1970. The law states that

---

[7]These measures will be discussed in more detail in Chapter Two.

> The Secretary shall require, to the greatest extent feasible, the employment of new and improved technologies, methods, and materials in housing construction, rehabilitation, and maintenance . . . with a view to reducing costs, and shall encourage and promote the acceptance and application of such advanced technology, methods, and materials by all segments of the housing industry. . . .[8]

Beyond this congressional directive, federal agencies have also invested in housing-related R&D and innovation because they were recognized as a legitimate strategy for pursuing their agency missions and goals. For example, the U.S. Department of Energy (DOE) has worked to increase energy efficiency in the home, the Department of Housing and Urban Development (HUD) has sought to make homes more affordable by lowering the cost of building materials and housing production, and the U.S. Environmental Protection Agency (EPA) has done research to reduce indoor health risks (e.g., lead poisoning, radon, air pollution).

Over the years, these and other agency efforts have had some success in supporting the early phases of the innovation process, such as conducting research and expanding the knowledge base, but they have generally been less successful at encouraging the adoption and diffusion of those innovations throughout the housing industry. Unfortunately, until new innovations are steadily developed, adopted, and diffused, their benefits will accumulate only slowly. Hence, the housing industry, government policymakers, and others continue to ask if the federal government could play a more productive role in supporting and accelerating the housing innovation system as a whole so that new technologies are not only developed but also commercialized and widely adopted throughout the industry.

OBJECTIVE OF THE STUDY

The primary objective of this study is to show how the federal government can more effectively support and accelerate innovation in housing by better understanding the industry *as it exists* and how it interacts with the innovation process. To this end, the study

---

[8]U.S. Congress (1970).

- defines innovation and explains the innovation process,

- describes the industry and explains how its characteristics influence the innovation process,

- reviews federal efforts intended to promote innovation,

- summarizes the tools available to the federal government to promote innovation, and

- recommends federal actions to support and accelerate innovation within the current industry structure.

METHODOLOGY

To fulfill these objectives, this study combines past RAND research with an extensive literature review and meetings with representatives from throughout the housing industry.

The project team built on prior RAND analysis on housing, innovation, federal research and development, and public-private partnerships. In earlier work, RAND conducted roundtable discussions on the adoption of information technology in the construction process and within the home. RAND also studied federally sponsored R&D related to buildings and housing. Most of the team's directly applicable knowledge resulted from RAND's assistance with technology roadmapping efforts conducted through the Partnership for Advancing Technology in Housing (PATH). RAND publications from the team's prior housing-related efforts include the following:

Scott Hassell, Scott Florence, and Emile Ettedgui, *Summary of Federal Construction, Building, and Housing Related Research & Development in FY1999*, Santa Monica, Calif.: RAND, MR-1390-HUD/NIST, 2001.

Rosalind Lewis, *Information Technology in the Home: Barriers, Opportunities, and Research Directions*, Santa Monica, Calif.: RAND, IP-203-OSTP, 2000.

Scott Hassell, Mark Bernstein, and Aimee Bower, *The Role of Information Technology in Housing Design and Construction*, Santa Monica, Calif.: RAND, CF-156-OSTP, 2000.

Our extensive literature review included publications on innovation, technology, housing, and homebuilding. We obtained them from the RAND library and electronic journals, via the Internet, and from libraries of the U.S. Department of Housing and Urban Development, and the National Association of Home Builders (NAHB) Research Center among others. Most of these sources were published in the United States over the past three decades. They include reports prepared by federal agencies, private firms, and nonprofit research organizations; articles from peer-reviewed journals; and meeting and workshop proceedings.

The authors interviewed industry experts, researchers, and government officials to verify and supplement insights gained from previous RAND research on housing innovation, as well as information on experiences with innovation and recent unpublished activities.[9]

REPORT ORGANIZATION

This report consists of six chapters. Following this introductory chapter, Chapters Two through Six address steps outlined in the study objective.

Chapter One presents the objectives, methodology, and structure of the study.

Chapter Two briefly introduces the state of innovation in U.S. housing; defines innovation, invention, and technology; presents the innovation process; and sets the stage for discussing how innovation fits within the context of the industry.

Chapter Three presents an overview of the housing industry by providing a background on how homes are designed, built, and sold, as well as the on roles and contributions of the industry's many participants.

Chapter Four examines the characteristics and motives that affect innovation in the industry.

---

[9]Discussions were held with representatives or former representatives of the U.S. Department of Housing and Urban Development, the U.S. Department of Energy, the National Institute for Standards and Technology, the NAHB Research Center, and DuPont among others.

Chapter Five presents an overview of federal involvement in promoting innovation in general and in the housing industry in particular. The chapter describes the complementary efforts of investing in R&D, passing legislation, and creating industry-specific programs to support innovation.

Chapter Six presents, analyzes, and recommends policy options that are available to the executive and legislative branches to support and accelerate innovation in housing.

Chapter Two

THE CONCEPT OF INNOVATION IN THE U.S. HOUSING INDUSTRY

THE STATE OF INNOVATION IN HOUSING

Much of the literature on innovation in housing examines the rate at which inventions are developed, how quickly innovations are diffused, and whether industry productivity is increasing.[1] Unfortunately, the conclusions of these studies are limited by a lack of data and the difficulty involved in collecting such data. As a result, conclusions are often based on small sample sizes or anecdotal experiences that cannot be extrapolated to industrywide analyses or cross-sector comparisons. Although it would be desirable to quantify the state of innovation, it is important to recognize that innovation, no matter its rate, is good, because improvement in products and services is associated with general levels of innovation. For this reason, this report explores how innovation can be increased.

Past housing innovation studies have also sought to increase innovation. Many of them identify characteristics of the industry as "barriers" to innovation.[2] In doing so, these studies have implied and sometimes concluded that the industry must be restructured to

---

[1]Studies finding that innovations are developed and diffused more slowly in housing than in other industries include NAHB Research Center et al. (1989); and Civil Engineering Research Foundation (1995a). However, other studies find that innovation and productivity trends in housing are not unlike trends in other industries. For example, see Slaughter (1993); and Rosefielde and Mills (1979).

[2]Examples of such barriers include the industry's highly competitive, fragmented, and regulated nature.

remove or lower these barriers for the rate of innovation to increase. As will be described below, history shows that imposing such massive change in the housing industry would be difficult, costly, and unlikely to succeed. A more constructive approach to promoting innovation is to consider the characteristics that define the housing industry and to focus on how innovation can be promoted *within* the existing industry. This is the approach used in this study. Thus, the first step in exploring how to promote innovation within this context is to develop an understanding of both the innovation process and the housing industry. This chapter provides an introduction to the first of these tasks by defining key terms, explaining the innovation process, and providing a structure within which to examine how and why innovations develop and spread.

DEFINITIONS

Key terms and their definitions in this report are listed below.

- *Knowledge* is an idea, fact, or principle that is known to one or more people.

- *Technology* is knowledge of a technical nature (e.g., physical laws and material properties). It encompasses the scientific method and material used to achieve a commercial or industrial objective. For example, it includes knowledge of how to manufacture, use, and evaluate products. It is not a product or process itself but the underlying "how-to."

- An *innovation* is a product, process, or other application of technology that is perceived as new by the user and advances the state of the art. Over time, an innovation may be adopted by many users and lose its novelty.

- The *innovation process* is one by which innovations are created and diffused. It may be accidental or the result of careful planning. The process is also affected by market demand, by technological capability, and by the participants involved.

- An *invention* is a new idea that fills a need or potential need better than any existing option. It can be an invention in the classic sense in that it is something entirely new or it can be a new application of an existing idea or a reintroduction of an out-of-use idea (for example, putting wheels on travel luggage). Invention is the first step in the innovation process, although an invention may not necessarily become a widely adopted innovation.

THE STANDARD MODEL: INNOVATION AS A LINEAR PROCESS

The innovation process has been studied extensively. Perhaps the most common conclusion from these studies is captured by Kline and Rosenberg (1986): "the systems used in innovation processes are among the most complex known (both technically and socially)." To better understand these processes, scholars routinely use conceptual models to explain the most important aspects of the innovation process even though no model could ever capture its full complexity. It is through the development, analysis, and comparison of model results to reality that the innovation process becomes better understood.

The most commonly used model of the innovation process is the linear model (see Figure 2.1). This model consists of several stages in sequence (i.e., the first stage is followed directly by the second phase, the second by the third, and so on). In this model, the innovation process consists of four such phases: research, development, demonstration, and deployment.[3] These four phases as well as their sequential ordering have led some to refer to this linear progression as the RDDD pipeline, or RD3 pipeline for short.

In this model, the innovation process begins with *researching* a problem and inventing a solution conceptually if not physically. Once an invention is found, it is refined and perfected through the *development* process. This could involve developing a small-scale or

RAND*MR1658-2.1*

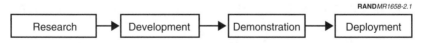

Figure 2.1—A Linear Model of the Innovation Process

---

[3]Recent uses of the linear RD3 model can be found in President's Committee of Advisors on Science and Technology (PCAST) (1999); and Bernstein and Lemer (1996).

prototype product that provides a proof-of-concept that the innovation is technologically sound.

The *demonstration* stage involves producing a full-scale prototype to prove not only the innovation's technical viability but also that it meets required safety standards, appeals to consumers, and can be produced at a reasonable cost. (This stage is also frequently called demonstration/evaluation because independent evaluation and testing organizations test the product to certify it as safe and effective.)

The final step in the innovation process is *deployment*. Sometimes referred to as the diffusion, commercialization, or marketing stage, this stage generally consists of increasing the production or manufacture of the innovation and making it commercially available. The outcome of this phase depends heavily on consumer demand, the cost of the product, regulatory acceptance, marketing efforts, and the cost and performance of competing products among other considerations.[4]

A BETTER MODEL

The clarity and simplicity of the linear model have led to its wide use in innovation studies and policy research, including those focused on housing and construction. Although popular at one time, the linear model is no longer held in high regard.[5] Some of its limitations are general and some are more housing-specific.

The model's limitations are presented below to help illustrate the complexities of innovation and the unique attributes of innovation in housing. With this discussion as a basis, the RAND research team has constructed a new model for innovation in the housing industry—one that aims to address the shortcomings in the linear model.

---

[4]The four-stage linear model is only one of many conceptually similar models. Discussions of other linear and nonlinear models can be found in Kline and Rosenberg (1986); Bijker et al. (1987); and Lutz and Salem (1995).

[5]These limitations do not mean the linear model is faulty. Recall that like all models, it is an approximation of reality rather than reality itself. A model's usefulness depends on its ability to explain behavior under specific circumstances. In many of the cases where the linear model is used, it is sufficient to explain important concepts and relationships.

In the subsequent chapters, this model will be used to explain how the innovation process could be better supported.

Industry-Independent Limitations

The most common criticism is that the real-world innovation process bears little resemblance to the highly structured linear model, because the conceptual stages represented in the linear model are neither discrete nor conducted in a strictly linear fashion. Rather, in many cases the conceptual phases occur concurrently and with significant feedback and cross-fertilization.[6] As interactions and iterations occur, real-world innovations are generally refined by additional research, technological capabilities, consumer preferences, markets, and other factors. Indeed, "tuning" an innovation so that it resonates with technical and market factors is often necessary for an innovation to be successfully deployed.

The path through the innovation process may be highly circuitous and indirect. Therefore, an invention's ultimate application and market may be much different than originally conceived.[7] For this reason, a 1997 presidential advisory body on science and technology stated that the linear model

> no longer works well and can even be seriously counterproductive. Rather than a pipeline, a more realistic image today might be a complex tapestry, with the various stages—basic science, applied

---

[6]See President's Committee of Advisors on Science and Technology (PCAST) (1999); and Bernstein and Lemer (1996).

[7]A housing-related example of this phenomenon is DuPont's Tyvek® Homewrap®. Tyvek is a tough, durable sheeting product that acts as a barrier to cold and warm air as well as water, but it allows water vapor to pass through. As a result, Tyvek is particularly well suited to improving the energy efficiency of homes while avoiding a number of problems related to moisture. However, Tyvek was not originally developed for the housing market. Its original application was as a protectant for new carpets in shipment. During the energy crises of the 1970s, however, an inventive homebuilder experimented with Tyvek to see if it could improve the energy efficiency of homes. As a result of the builder's success and significant product development efforts by DuPont, Tyvek is now used throughout the construction industry. Parry Norling, RAND, personal communication, December 17, 2001.

research, development, demonstration, commercialization—all strongly entangled and inseparable throughout the process.[8]

A similar conclusion was reached by a recently completed U.S. Department of Energy review conducted at the request of the Bush administration's National Energy Policy.[9]

Another critique of the linear model focuses on the role of research in the innovation process. Namely, the idea that innovation is initiated by research-induced scientific understanding is frequently wrong. Inventions are often conceived and developed using knowledge that the inventor already possesses, and, in many cases, invention occurs despite a lack of understanding of the underlying scientific and technical principles. In these cases, innovation results from intuition, experimentation, and trial-and-error rather than from rigorous theoretical understanding.[10]

Next, the uncertain and exploratory nature of research often means that the resulting knowledge may be of limited use in addressing the original goal. However, this research, presuming it is shared with others, adds to society's larger base of knowledge, thereby aiding the larger innovation system.

Finally, just as a lack of technical knowledge can stop the innovation process, so too can nontechnical considerations. For example, a lack of consumer interest, weak market demand, or high costs can all stop an innovation. In addition, innovations can be stopped if they are incompatible with or threaten established technologies, companies, or cultural factors.

---

[8]President's Committee of Advisors on Science and Technology (PCAST) (1997, pp. 7–14).

[9] U.S. Department of Energy (2002, pp. 5-3 to 5-5). These limitations are also recognized by scholars. See, for example, Kline and Rosenberg (1986, p. 286): "The linear model distorts the reality of innovation in several ways, and most serious students of innovation have now come to recognize those distortions. However, improved models have not yet come into widespread use. Consequently, the linear model is still often invoked in current discussions, particularly in political discussions."

[10]For example, if rigorous understanding was required to harness scientific principles, many innovations from the bicycle to surgical procedures would not exist.

Housing-Specific Limitations to the Linear Model

Beyond these industry-independent limitations, the linear model also has significant shortfalls when applied to the housing industry. In many ways, these limitations are an artifact of early innovation studies that sought to explain the development of complex science and technology such as the atomic bomb, radar, jet engines, and semiconductors. In most of these cases, the federal government requested, funded, and intended to purchase the end product. As a result, the linear model of innovation was developed within the context of

- large, integrated firms with advanced R&D programs,

- relatively abundant funding for research, development, and demonstration, and

- a nearly guaranteed large and sustained market.

Given this context, it is not surprising that the linear model was developed and that it was relatively successful at explaining the innovation process under these circumstances. However, the industrial characteristics that are embedded in the linear model diverge from those of the housing industry in a number of ways.

First, the housing industry is fragmented vertically, horizontally, and geographically. Also, unlike the groundbreaking and inherently innovative projects that led to the linear model, innovations in the housing industry are often resisted. For example, a recent report by the National Research Council (2001, p. 25) evaluated energy-related research funded by the U.S. Department of Energy and found that

> Although many energy-efficient materials and products do not have higher first costs, builders resist implementing them because additional time is needed to train workers to install them. Also, until the builder gains experience with these energy-efficient materials and products, they are perceived as risky.

These and other observations that will be elaborated on in Chapter Three suggest that the linear model of innovation is less effective for housing than it may be for other industries.

The Expanded Nonlinear Model of Housing Innovation

Since the linear model is not able to explain many aspects of innovation in the housing industry, this study sought a model that better addresses the unique characteristics of that industry. Although the innovation literature provides several alternative models, none was ideal for the purposes of this study. After reviewing these studies and given our insights into the housing industry, we created a new model that included the best features of others yet was simple enough to inform the policymaking process about ways to better support and accelerate housing innovation.[11] Our model is presented in Figure 2.2.

The most significant change in this model is that within the familiar left-to-right progression, *research* has been replaced with *invention*. This change reflects that the first step of the innovation process is a new idea, or at least an idea that is new to the inventor. In this model, the new idea is referred to as an invention. Decoupling invention from research more accurately reflects that research does not automatically lead to inventions; rather the inventor's thinking is usually prompted by curiosity or some other external trigger. As a

RAND*MR1658-2.2*

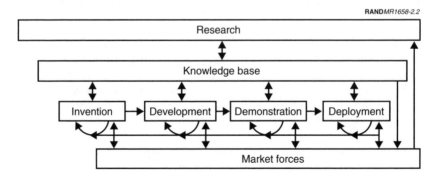

Figure 2.2—Our Model of the Innovation Process

---

[11]We found the "chain-linked model" to be especially useful; however, an alternative representation of the market forces made the model more useful to this study. See Kline and Rosenberg (1986, p. 290).

result of the substitution of invention for research, the familiar left-to-right progression will now be referred to by the acronym ID3.

Other major changes in this model are that *research, knowledge,* and *market forces* influence the ID3 progression at every stage. The placement of *research* and *knowledge base* reflect that research typically leads to knowledge rather than directly to invention. Similarly, it shows that when the knowledge base is not sufficient to allow the ID3 phases to progress, an innovation stops until new research extends the available knowledge. The last major change to the model is the addition of *market forces.* Adding market forces reflects the need for funding to finance the ID3 process, to create consumer demand for the ultimate product, and to ensure that the product meets regulatory requirements and can be readily deployed.

Finally, this model also resolves the feedback and interaction limitations inherent in the linear model. Feedback occurs within and between every stage of the ID3 process. In addition, the two-headed arrows represent constant interplay and feedback among the ID3 process, the technical knowledge base, and market forces.

Through these changes, the expanded nonlinear model preserves much of the simplicity of the linear model while more accurately explaining how research, knowledge, and market forces influence the overall pace of innovation. As a result, it provides a better framework for examining innovation in the housing industry. However, several additional aspects of innovation merit further review, namely, how participants in the process affect innovation-related decisions as well as what their motivations are for supporting and adopting innovation.

MOTIVATIONS FOR SUPPORTING AND ADOPTING INNOVATION

What factors inspire homebuilders, homeowners, product manufacturers, and others to invent, design, or adopt innovations? Previous studies have identified and classified various motives.[12] Although

---

[12]Mitropoulos and Tatum (1995); and Rosenberg (1976).

individual categories differ by author, the three most useful distinctions we found in the literature included the following:

- *Seeking Competitive Advantage.* Decisionmakers may support or adopt an innovation to obtain an advantage over their competitors. Doing so may help differentiate their product, lower their costs, or raise their profits. Understandably, as more firms adopt an innovation, the advantage accruing to each firm is diminished, meaning that the innovation often effectively becomes a requirement.

- *Improving Technological Efficiency.* The ability to improve efficiency can motivate a decisionmaker to adopt an innovation even when there is no clear need but because it will likely lead to a better product or service. Since this motivation is not driven by need, the innovation may be resisted until the decisionmaker can obtain enough information to assess its risks.

- *Meeting External Requirements.* Finally, external requirements can force a decisionmaker to involuntarily support or adopt an innovation. For example, a homebuilder may be forced to use an innovation because of a change in the building code or because a homeowner insists that the innovation be used.

Figure 2.3 compares the direction and intensity of a given motivation as a function of time. In other words, it shows whether a given motivation is a force for or against innovation and whether its intensity increases or decreases over time. In addition, it shows how a motivation overlaps with a generic "S-shaped" diffusion curve.

By definition, innovations start on the left of the graph with no diffusion. They are then willingly adopted by firms seeking to obtain competitive advantage. Early on, those who might be interested in adopting an innovation for reasons of technological efficiency are deterred by a lack of information. Finally, after a moderate level of diffusion, the available information causes those who were formerly risk-averse to adopt the innovation solely to improve technological efficiency. A short time later, as the innovation comes into wider use, the innovation becomes a requirement meaning that diffusion is further driven by external requirements.

RAND*MR1658-2.3*

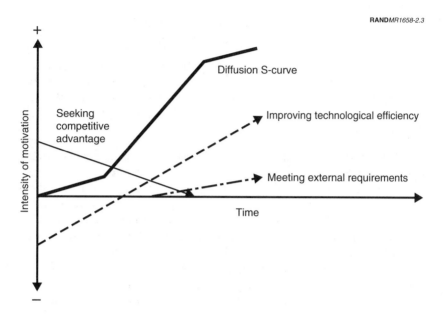

SOURCE: Adapted from Mitropoulos and Tatum (1995, p. 22).

Figure 2.3—Forces for Adoption and Diffusion over Time

Although neither motivations nor diffusion needs to follow these specific trends, this diagram helps illustrate the various motivations for adopting an innovation and how each may influence the thought processes of decisionmakers. However, even these motivations do not fully explain decisions to support or adopt innovation. Additional factors used to make these decisions are discussed in the next section.

DECISIONMAKING IN THE INNOVATION PROCESS

Whether an invention successfully passes through the entire innovation process depends on the cumulative decisions of many hundreds of people and organizations. To begin to understand how these decisions are made, consider the simple agent-based model shown in

Figure 2.4.[13] This model provides a simplified but useful introduction to how innovations are evaluated and whether they are adopted.

The central participant in the model is the *decision agent*. This person decides whether to support or adopt an innovation. In this model, decision agents make decisions about innovations after an evaluation of risks, rewards, and motivations as well as two additional resources.

The first additional resource is their knowledge base—decisionmakers can consider only innovations that they know to exist. Their second resource is input from those seeking to influence their decision. Known as *influence agents*, these participants try to influence the decision agent's evaluation of risks, rewards, and motivations. For example, an influence agent might encourage the use of an innovation by demonstrating its benefits, by providing incentives to the decisionmaker, or by modifying the constraints or limitations facing the decision agent. The third and final participant involved in the decision process is the *enabling agent*. This participant expands the

RAND*MR1658-2.4*

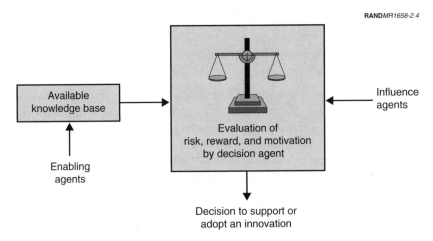

Figure 2.4—Participants and the Innovation Process

---

[13]The model prepared for this report was inspired by NAHB Research Center et al. (1989); NAHB Research Center (2001c); and Ventre (1979). Readers should note that the general ideas presented are also found in HUD literature on housing economics.

decisionmaker's knowledge base through invention and research and by accessing the knowledge produced by others and sharing it with the decision agent. Thus, although it is tempting to place the greatest responsibility for using an innovation on the decision agent, this model suggests that influence and enabling agents can have a significant effect on innovation decisions.

As will be described in the following chapters, this agent-based model of decisionmaking helps explain the difficulties involved in successfully completing the innovation process. Although specific examples will be discussed in the next chapter, the housing industry's professional, geographical, and regulatory fragmentation[14] mean that successfully introducing an innovation throughout the country potentially requires that many thousands of people become aware of the innovation (i.e., add it to their knowledge base) and choose to use it and even to recommend it to others (i.e., to the decision agent or the influence agent).

In the context of the housing industry, the homeowner is ideally the ultimate decision agent, but he or she often receives guidance from homebuilders and designers (who act as enabling and influence agents). Similarly, homebuilders and designers often rely on suppliers, salesman, and subcontractors for information about new products and how to choose among them when they purchase building materials. From these examples alone, it should be clear that successfully developing and deploying an innovation requires that many industry participants learn about and accept the innovation. Beyond this challenge, the decision process can be further slowed and influenced by imperfect understanding of others' preferences, breakdowns in communication, and intentional or unintentional biases.

Social and Historical Dimensions to Innovation

The bulk of this discussion has focused on the economic dimensions that affect innovation decisions, but these are not the only forces that affect participants' decisions. An extensive literature by sociologists and historical anthropologists also argues that participants make de-

---

[14]For a discussion of the regulatory system and the challenges it poses to new technology see National Evaluation Service (forthcoming).

cisions within a particular historical context or "technological frame." In other words, a participant's time, place, past experiences, and professional training shape how he or she thinks about technology and housing.[15]

For example, homes in the United States generally consist of bedrooms, bathrooms, living rooms, and kitchens built from wood, concrete, brick, and other familiar materials. As a result, decisionmakers have firmly established concepts of what a home should be. This means that housing types and innovations that stretch this concept too far may not be invented or supported through the innovation process. A decisionmaker may consciously or subconsciously be constrained by his or her historical context or technological frame.[16]

Within this view of explaining decisionmaking, it is important to realize that both enabling and influence agents play important roles in expanding the decision agent's frame so that they may consider new ideas in a broader and less biased fashion.

Participants in the Deployment Phase

In the case of the housing industry, most individuals participating in the innovation process are involved in the deployment phase. As will be described in the next chapter, a single innovation may involve hundreds of thousands of firms and even millions of individuals who act as independent decision agents. Also, since most participants are focused on building and maintaining quality homes at low cost and at low risk to themselves, innovation is not a priority in and of itself. As a result, motivating deployment phase decisionmakers to use an innovation can be quite difficult.

---

[15]Bijker et al. (1987).

[16]For example, several features of houses that we take for granted, such as closets or a separate room containing a bathtub, sink, and toilet, were not included in homes until the 19th century and were not commonplace until the 20th. Before this time, different ideas of the concept of privacy and what constituted a house prevented such features from being viewed as appropriate. See Rybczynski (1986).

Participants in the Invention, Development, and Demonstration Phases

Finally, it is important to realize that the agent-based decision model also applies throughout the invention, development, and demonstration phases. However, rather than decision agents evaluating products or building materials, decision agents decide among ideas. Also, instead of homeowners and homebuilders being the decision agents, influence agents, and enabling agents, it is researchers, managers, and investors who make decisions, seek to influence decisions, and increase the knowledge base. In fact, during the first three phases of the innovation process, inventors, researchers, managers, and investors each play the various roles of decision agent, enabling agent, and influence agent as research, knowledge, and market forces are harnessed to bring an invention through to deployment.

APPLYING INNOVATION CONCEPTS TO HOUSING

This chapter has introduced the state of innovation in housing, the innovation process, the motivations for supporting and adopting innovations, as well as how participants decide whether innovations are supported and adopted. This information provides important background for the following chapters that will introduce the housing industry in more detail. In so doing, the reader will be able to see how the industry's own processes and characteristics create additional challenges for innovation. This will set the stage for more detailed discussions of past efforts to promote innovation as well as how innovation might be better supported and accelerated in the future.

Chapter Three

THE U.S. HOUSING INDUSTRY AS THE CONTEXT FOR INNOVATION

WHAT IS THE U.S. HOUSING INDUSTRY?

The housing industry comprises hundreds of thousands of firms designing, building, and maintaining the nation's homes. It is also made up of millions of individuals working in roughly 80 capacities ranging from surveyors to bankers, Realtors, product manufacturers, code inspectors, homebuilders, contractors, insurance agents, homebuyers, and many others.[1] Harvard University's Joint Center for Housing Studies has estimated that the housing sector, in total, represents roughly 20 percent of gross domestic product (GDP) once all housing-related costs have been included.[2] If one only looks at residential construction, it alone has averaged four percent of GDP over the last 20 years.[3] Finally, the housing industry produces the most valuable asset a family owns as well as the largest component of the nation's physical wealth.[4]

---

[1]O'Brien et al. (2000).

[2]Joint Center for Housing Studies of Harvard University (2002, p. 6).

[3]For the period 1981 to 2000, residential housing investments expressed as a percentage of GDP have an annual average of 4.1 percent. U.S. Department of Commerce (2002).

[4]In 2000, residential structures represented 36 percent of the value of the nation's fixed assets. Of privately held assets, residential structures represented 49.5 percent. U.S. Department of Commerce (2002).

The size, complexity, and many facets of the housing industry make a complete yet simple description of the industry nearly impossible. To overcome this, we use the general chronology involved in building a single-family home to structure our discussion of the housing industry. We use this systematic approach even for industry participants far removed from the construction site, by introducing them in the phase where they have their most significant effect on the home-building process.

We also simplify this introduction by focusing it on single-family homes—the largest portion of the market. Although this limits the explicit discussion of other forms of residential construction (e.g., high-rises, manufactured homes), this report's analysis and conclusions can provide insights into other forms of housing as well. Before describing the housing industry through the process of building a single-family home, we briefly review the nation's housing stock and current construction trends to show the historical and continuing importance of single-family homes.

HOUSING STOCK, NEW CONSTRUCTION, AND REMODELING

In 1999, there were roughly 115 million units of housing in the United States.[5] Of these, 68 percent were single-family homes, 25 percent were multifamily, and 7 percent were HUD-Code homes.[6] In that same year, 1.6 million new site-built[7] homes were con-

---

[5]U.S. Department of Commerce and U.S. Department of Housing and Urban Development (2000).

[6]A HUD-Code home is a housing unit designed to be towed on its own chassis, with transportation gear integral to the unit when it leaves the factory. They are produced in factories and transported virtually completed to site. They are known as HUD-Code homes because, as products of interstate commerce, they are regulated by a national—rather than local—building code that is maintained by the U.S. Department of Housing and Urban Development. HUD-Code homes do not include travel trailers, motor homes, or modular housing though they are often confused with those types of housing.

[7]A site-built home is largely built on-site from basic materials (e.g., plywood, lumber, concrete block) and building components (e.g., roof trusses, wall sections, kitchen cabinets). Site-built homes can also be built from housing modules.

structed with 80 percent being single-family and 20 percent being multifamily.[8] In addition to site-built homes, 338,300 HUD-Code homes were placed throughout the United States.[9]

In addition to new construction, remodeling, maintenance, and repairs are also an important part of the housing industry. For example, in 1999 the U.S. Census Bureau estimates that $143 billion—35 percent of all investments in fixed residential property—were spent for these purposes.[10] During the 1990s, roughly 70 percent of these expenditures were for improvements (e.g., additions, alterations, and major replacements) with the remainder being maintenance and repair (see Figure 3.1).[11]

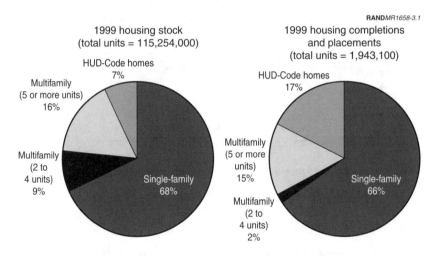

Figures 3.1—Housing Stock and Housing Completions, 1999

---

[8]U.S. Department of Commerce and U.S. Department of Housing and Urban Development (2001).

[9]U.S. Census Bureau (2002b).

[10]U.S. Census Bureau (2001b).

[11]U.S. Census Bureau (2001b).

OVERVIEW OF THE HOMEBUILDING PROCESS

The housing construction process can be divided into five stages, beginning with land development and then moving to design, pre-construction, construction, and post-construction (see Figure 3.2).[12]

This model of the extended homebuilding process is sufficient for our purposes, but it does not include every participant, every activity, and every case of feedback and interaction. This is partly because not all participants or activities in a given phase are relevant to every home, but also this simplification is intended to keep the explanation clear and useful.[13] This means that the roles of homeowners or homebuilders who are active in many and potentially all steps are typically described only in the stage where they are most involved.

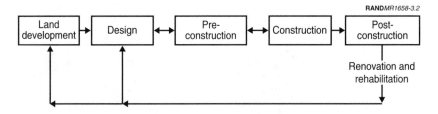

Figure 3.2—The Homebuilding Process

LAND DEVELOPMENT

Land development is usually the first step in the homebuilding process because whether the home is built on an empty lot in an existing neighborhood or on undeveloped land, a number of steps must be completed before construction of the home (see Figure 3.3).

---

[12]These five stages as well as the "exploded" diagrams and the discussion on the following pages are adapted from the following sources, except where indicated: NAHB Research Center (2001b); and Hassell et al. (2000).

[13]For example, the precise ordering of some activities will depend on when the homebuyer becomes involved in the homebuilding process (i.e., during land development, design, or post-construction).

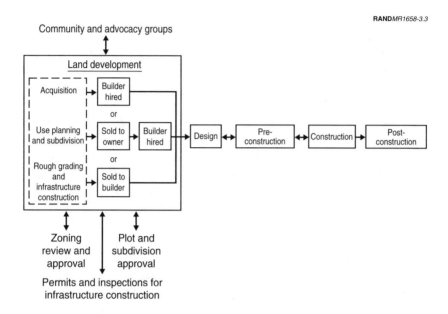

Figure 3.3—The Land Development Stage

In a new community, a land developer may purchase a large parcel of land on which to build a number of homes or may subdivide the land and sell individual lots to homebuilders or homebuyers. After acquisition, the land developer must obtain regulatory approvals for the land's intended use, portions of the land must graded (i.e., leveled or contoured), and basic infrastructure installed (e.g., water, sewer, electricity, roads).

In the case of a lot purchased in an existing neighborhood, some or all of these steps may have been completed. Even rehabilitating or renovating existing homes may require land development activities if the use of the property or the existing structure is to be changed significantly.

Among the participants in the land development stage are developers, municipal planning and zoning departments, elected officials, and community interest and advocacy groups.

- *Developers* buy land to develop into residential property. The land purchased might be undeveloped property or lots with existing structures. In some cases, developers are directly involved in homebuilding, taking loans from financial institutions to build new homes or to rehabilitate existing structures. In other cases, developers obtain needed permits, install basic infrastructure (e.g., water, sewer, electricity, roads), and then sell individual lots.

  In the case of new communities, developers also often have the opportunity to establish architectural and neighborhood covenants that add additional requirements beyond those of the municipality. These covenants are typically used to impose standards for home appearances and lot use.[14]

- *Planning and zoning departments and elected officials* together develop, enforce, and modify land-use and zoning policies for their jurisdictions. The role of planning and zoning departments is to enforce existing land-use regulations and to provide elected officials with plans, advice, and assistance in developing, enforcing, and modifying those regulations. As a result of the largely advisory role of planning and zoning departments, it is the elected officials who ultimately accept, reject, or modify their suggestions and rule on major land development issues.

- *Community interest groups* often seek to influence land-use and development decisions through public comment, advocacy, and technical support. These groups are generally locally based and they represent various causes ranging from affordable housing to environmental protection, historical preservation, and architectural features and appearances among others. Although usually not directly involved in individual homes, they may influence the decisions and actions of developers and municipal agencies. In addition, affordable housing interest groups may provide labor or economic incentives for land development, construction, and homeownership.

---

[14]In some cases, covenants can directly affect whether innovations such as solar arrays are permitted or whether a homeowner is entitled to solar access.

DESIGN

Designing a home can vary from using an "off-the-shelf" plan to custom designing an entire home from scratch. In the case of off-the-shelf plans, licensed architects and engineers may only need to review and approve plan revisions made by draftsmen. However, licensed architects and engineers may be intimately involved in designing a custom home. Beyond the architectural and engineering plans, the design process also includes specifying basic materials, products, and systems, as well as rough cost estimates. The above-described design stage for building a new home is also the first step when a home is remodeled (or more generally rehabilitated).

In addition, for the purposes of this study, the design phase of the homebuilding process also includes the many "upstream" efforts that directly influence how homes are designed and which products and materials architects and engineers can use. This upstream work, done by companies, universities, governments, and nonprofit organizations, includes product and process research, consumer and market research, design, testing, and evaluation (see Figure 3.4).

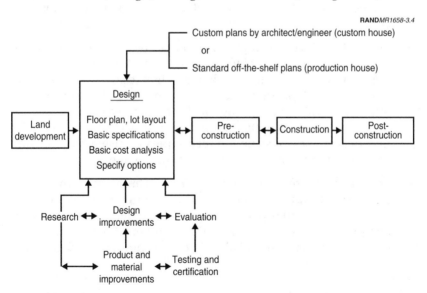

Figure 3.4—The Design Stage

The participants directly involved in the design phase include the following:

- *Architects and Engineers.* Architects focus mainly on the overall appearance and design of a home, whereas engineers typically prepare general designs for the structural, mechanical (i.e., plumbing, heating, and air conditioning), and electrical systems. Since many homes have simple designs and may be modifications of pre-existing designs, the architect and engineer involvement may be limited to approving plans prepared by others (e.g., draftsmen). In contrast, for new and complex home designs, architects and engineers may be involved in nearly every aspect of the design.

- *Homebuyers.* In situations where homebuyers purchase an empty lot and initiate the construction of a new home, they will become involved in the design stage.[15] Their level of involvement will vary depending on the level of customization as well as on how much they defer to the judgment of the designers. In addition, depending on the particular owner, they might stay involved in all of the subsequent phases of the homebuilding process.

- *Researchers.* The housing-related research community is very diverse and consists of scientists, engineers, and others from industry, government, and academia. They research new building materials and products ranging from roof shingles to prefabricated wall sections and washing machines among others. They also study the homebuilding process itself and recommend new design and construction techniques for using both old and new products to lower costs and improve quality.

- *Testing and Certification Organizations.* These organizations test and certify products and materials according to procedures and criteria that standard-setting bodies have determined will protect public safety and ensure minimum performance. It is their role to independently and objectively test products and materials

---

[15]Homebuyers have the most variable role of all participants. They can enter the homebuilding process at any stage. For this reason, they may not be involved in design at all, or they may be very involved. In this report, the homebuyer is primarily discussed within the design stage.

according to these standards and to present their findings in official reports.[16]

- *Evaluation Groups.* These groups review new products and materials to determine under what conditions they comply with the nation's "model" building codes found in the United States.[17] To make this decision, evaluation groups review the innovation itself as well as the reports produced by testing and certification organizations. They then document and publish their findings. The resulting evaluation report provides an independent, advisory, and professional opinion on whether a new technology, perhaps under specific conditions, satisfies the requirements of the model codes. In practice, these reports are widely used by code officials, designers, and all others interested in the new technology.[18]

PRE-CONSTRUCTION

Planning for construction begins with choosing the homebuilder (also known as a general contractor) who in turn selects trade contractors (also known as subcontractors) and plans the related tasks including obtaining plan approvals and permits, contracting and scheduling work crews, and ordering and procuring materials.

Concurrent with these efforts, the design plans are reviewed by local building departments and other agencies such as fire and public works. These reviews ensure that the plans meet the codes adopted by state and local authorities. However, since these codes are themselves based on the "model codes," model code groups are also considered part of the pre-construction stage (see Figure 3.5).

---

[16]The standards used in these tests are typically directly referenced in the nation's building codes.

[17]Building codes and the "model codes" will be introduced in the next section of this chapter.

[18]Traditionally, each model code has its own evaluation service. However, on April 18, 2002, the International Code Council (ICC) announced that all existing evaluation services would be consolidated into a single evaluation service that will reside within the ICC. See www.nateval.org

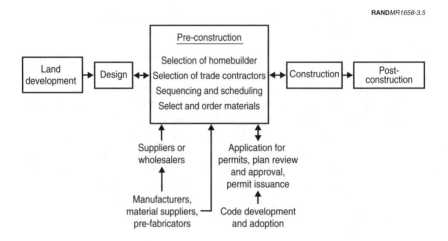

RAND*MR1658-3.5*

Figure 3.5—The Pre-Construction Stage

Finally, for the purposes of this study, this stage also includes the production and delivery to the construction site of the building materials and products used to construct the home itself. As a result, raw material producers, processors, and manufacturers are part of the pre-construction stage as are the retail and wholesale suppliers who provide the distribution system needed to deliver these goods to builders and trade contractors.

The primary participants in the pre-construction stage include homebuilders, model code organizations, municipal regulatory agencies, and the producers and suppliers of building materials and products. These are all discussed in more detail below, except for homebuilders, who will primarily be discussed in the next section.

- *Model Code Organizations.* Although state and local regulatory agencies are usually responsible for updating and enforcing building codes, these agencies rely on model code organizations[19] to produce complete, integrated, and up-to-date re-

---

[19]There are model code groups focused on building codes, electrical codes, fire codes, etc. Historically the United States had three major model building code organizations, each focused on a particular geographic region. These groups are the Building Officials and Code Administrators International, the International Conference of Building

quirements known as "model codes." Developed using theory, practice, and carefully designed voting procedures, states and localities use the model codes to guide the development of their own.

- *Regulatory Agencies.* Regulatory agencies have two major responsibilities: adopting codes and enforcing them. Depending on the law in a particular state, the responsibility for adopting and enforcing codes may rest with state or local agencies or may be shared by both. Many agencies adopt the model codes "as is," but others customize them to their own particular needs. Officials from regulatory agencies (e.g., building and fire departments) are responsible for enforcing these codes and determining whether plans and specified technologies comply.[20]

- *Material Producers, Product Manufacturers, and Pre-Fabricators.* Material producers obtain and produce the raw materials such as gypsum, asphalt, and wood that are then used to produce common building materials such as drywall, roof shingles, and doors. Material producers also provide many of the inputs such as steel, brass, and plastic that are used by product manufacturers to make items from water faucets to kitchen refrigerators. Finally, pre-fabricators process materials and intermediate products into larger subcomponents such as roof trusses and wall sections that can be more easily assembled on construction sites. Beyond producing these goods, producers also submit their products to testing, certifying, and evaluation organizations to document that they meet code in the hope that designers will specify them, builders will use them, and code officials will approve them.

- *Suppliers.* Finally, retail and wholesale suppliers are the primary channel through which homebuilders, trade contractors, and in some cases homeowners, learn about and order building mate-

---

Officials, and the Southern Building Code Congress International. In the mid-1990s, these three groups jointly founded an umbrella organization known as the International Code Council to develop a single set of comprehensive and coordinated model construction codes.

[20]Regulatory agencies enforce the codes through several mechanisms including reviewing construction documents and evaluation reports, issuing construction permits, inspecting construction sites, issuing occupancy certificates, and verifying that buildings are maintained in a safe manner. For an overview of the building codes and how they affect new technology, see National Evaluation Service (forthcoming).

rials and products. In many cases, suppliers specialize by trade or product and they generally order directly from the manufacturer.

CONSTRUCTION

Construction of the home consists of managing labor and materials, preparing the land and foundation, erecting and enclosing the walls and roof, installing the mechanical and electrical systems, installing appliances, and applying the interior and exterior finishes and trim.[21] During these steps, the builder and trade contractors obtain additional permits from municipal regulatory departments. In addition, field inspectors from these departments conduct site inspections to ensure that the construction is in compliance with the local codes and requirements. The home construction stage typically ends with the issuance of the certificate of use and occupancy, which is awarded after a home successfully passes the final inspections by municipal authorities (see Figure 3.6).

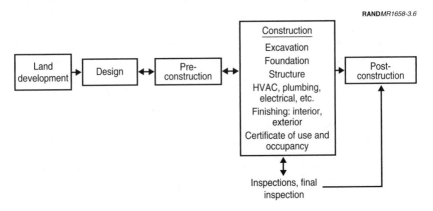

Figure 3.6—The Construction Stage

---

[21]Portions of this section are based on NAHB Research Center (1993). Readers interested in further discussion of the subprocesses, sequencing, and different approaches to managing work flows should refer to this reference.

The primary participants in this phase are the homebuilder, trade contractors, and municipal field inspectors.

- *Homebuilders.* As the central participants in the construction stage, homebuilders are responsible for all aspects of the physical construction of the home, from the foundation to the roof, including all wiring, plumbing, and detailing. Homebuilders may do all of these tasks themselves or subcontract them to trade contractors.

- *Trade Contractors*, also known as subcontractors, typically specialize in a specific trade. Examples include framers, electricians, roofers, and plumbers. These groups generally own their own tools and equipment and manage their own work crews when doing work for a homebuilder. Small and middle-size homebuilders, in particular, depend heavily on trade contractors.

- *Municipal Field Inspectors.* Building departments and other municipal agencies typically have field inspectors who make scheduled and unscheduled visits to construction sites to ensure that construction complies with local codes. Failure to comply typically requires replacing and reinspecting unsatisfactory work, thereby adding costs and delays.

POST-CONSTRUCTION

The post-construction stage consists of a variety of events, including marketing, checking legal requirements, and adding the finishing touches required to put homeowners or renters in their homes. First, if a home has not yet been sold, it must be marketed. Most buyers finance their purchase with a mortgage and buy an insurance policy. Smaller purchases that help finish the home are often added into the mortgage, including kitchen or laundry appliances and light fixtures. Also, before a home is occupied, minor repairs and corrections are frequently made as well as changes to meet the buyer or resident's needs and preferences. These purchases, repairs, and changes may require additional financing or coverage through warranty claims.

Finally, owners begin to incur a variety of operation and maintenance costs including monthly utilities (e.g., water, telephone, gas, and electricity) as well as larger but less frequent expenses such as reroofing, reflooring, and landscaping. The post-construction stage is also where remodeling efforts initiate, although in many cases, such efforts may lead back to the land development or design stages (see Figure 3.7).

Although roles and the degree of involvement vary considerably depending on the circumstances, some or all of the following participants may be involved in the post-construction stage:

- *Real estate agents and salespersons* market new or renovated homes to potential buyers. Independent Realtors as well as the sales agents of homebuilding firms are often the main contact for homebuyers. As such, they can be the most important source of information about a home and its surroundings for the homebuyer. Usually, these professionals are not involved in earlier stages of the home construction process and might know little about the technical details of materials, components, or the processes used in building a home (unless the salesperson is the homebuilder).

- *Mortgage brokers* evaluate whether a potential homebuyer can afford a given home. If so, they find appropriate financing options and loan sources at a primary lender. Mortgage brokers charge homebuyers fees for their services, and how much they

RAND*MR1658-3.7*

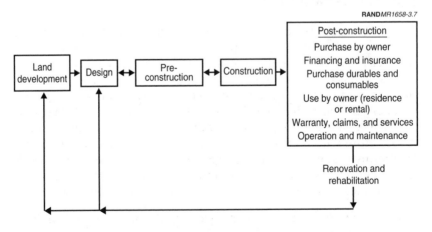

Figure 3.7—The Post-Construction Stage

charge can be affected by the costs involved in determining the value of a home and the creditworthiness of a loan applicant.

- *Appraisers* assess the value of a home to ensure that its value is at least as great as the requested loan. Appraisers estimate the value of a home by judging its structural integrity, material composition, size, location, and the value of adjacent and comparable homes among other factors. Appraisals based on these factors alone are referred to as "standard appraisals." A "custom appraisal" can be used to better recognize the value of homes with unique features that may be undervalued by a traditional appraisal. Since custom appraisals require special training and are more detailed, they typically take longer and are more expensive, increasing the cost to the homebuyer.

- *Primary lenders* evaluate the loan application and appraisal reports submitted by the mortgage brokers. If the application is approved, the primary lender makes the initial mortgage loan directly to the homebuyer. Primary lenders include savings and loans, commercial banks, mortgage companies, and state and local housing finance agencies. In some cases, primary lenders may then sell these mortgages to secondary lenders.

- *Secondary lenders* buy mortgages from primary lenders and package them together in bundles as low-risk investments that are then sold to insurance companies, securities dealers, and other financial institutions. The two largest secondary lenders are Fannie Mae and Freddie Mac.[22]

- *Insurers* provide homeowners with insurance coverage against the risk of fire or other damage to the home. Aside from the protection this offers to the buyer, mortgage lenders typically require that a homebuyer have insurance to ensure that the lender can recover the remaining portion of the loan in the event of loss.

---

[22]Secondary lenders play a large role in keeping housing affordable because they increase the supply of funds available for low-interest loans beyond what would otherwise be available. In addition, by purchasing mortgages from primary lenders, secondary lenders make it easier for primary lenders to finance other stages of the homebuilding process including land development and builder-initiated homes.

THE HOMEBUILDING PROCESS AND ITS IMPLICATIONS FOR INNOVATION

This brief description of the homebuilding process reveals that it is complex and requires careful coordination and sequencing of many tasks and specialized participants. Only when all of these parties are brought together in the correct order do their unique skills, materials, and services result in a quality home successfully purchased by a homebuyer.

Although this description of the homebuilding process and its participants may seem to fully explain how a home is built, this process is independent of the characteristics that shape the housing industry and how the homebuilding process is carried out. This process description also leaves out the motivations that guide the decisionmaking of the process's participants. Each of these is discussed in the next chapter.

Chapter Four

INDUSTRY CHARACTERISTICS AND MOTIVES AND THEIR EFFECT ON INNOVATION

The homebuilding process provides a useful structure to introduce the housing industry, but it does not fully explain the industry or its relationship with the innovation process. This chapter supplements Chapter Three by describing several of the industry's overarching characteristics, by providing insight into the motives of its participants, and by highlighting examples of innovations that are in various stages of realization.

INDUSTRY CHARACTERISTICS AND THEIR EFFECT ON INNOVATION

The U.S. housing industry is often described as competitive, cyclical, and fragmented, but what do these terms mean? What is the justification or evidence for these claims? What are the implications for innovation? This section answers these questions for the housing industry in general although, in many cases, discussion focuses on homebuilders in particular, because of their central role in making the decision to adopt an innovation. Nonetheless, this focus does not suggest that other participants are unimportant.

Low Barriers to Entry Make the Housing Industry Highly Competitive

The housing industry, and homebuilding in particular, are often described as highly competitive, because the industry's high fragmentation and low capital requirements make it relatively easy for firms to enter and exit.[1] For example, those seeking to start a homebuilding firm can borrow money to purchase land and materials and pay subcontractors. Since subcontractors provide their own tools and equipment, homebuilders increasingly focus on process management. Also, most builders, especially small builders, use similar methods to manage this process, and, therefore homebuilders often earn only a small to modest profit on each home. As a result, they have few earnings to invest in innovation-related investments.[2]

Although innovation researchers argue that competition leads firms to embrace innovation to differentiate their products, homebuilders often feel that learning about and installing innovations cost more than buyers are willing to pay. That said, some builders have been quite successful at using innovations to create a niche market for their services (e.g., energy-efficient builders). However, others argue that because of the ease of entering and exiting the market, builders avoid innovations that pose unnecessary risk, since a bad outcome might lead to an unhappy customer or future costs to remove the innovation and replace it with traditional materials. As a result, builders often describe themselves as risk-averse with respect to innovations to protect their reputation and reduce the chance of losing money or going bankrupt.[3]

Cyclical Business Cycles Lead to Low Investment in Employees and Training

As with the economy in general, the housing industry experiences cyclical changes in demand. However, its ups and downs have historically been steeper than those of the economy at large. In fact, by one measure, national investment in residential construction has

---

[1] NAHB Research Center et al. (1989, p. 19).

[2] Builders and other participants in the housing industry may finance innovation efforts through loans, equity, or debt. Depending on the type of business (i.e., proprietorship versus corporation) and its anticipated cash flows, the cost and risk of obtaining such financing may be undesirable.

[3] We would prefer to explain builder behavior by citing quantitative data but, as previously stated, there are few or no such data. For this reason, our insights are drawn from builders' self-assessments of their attitudes and decisions toward innovation even if they are potentially less accurate.

been 50 percent more variable than in the overall economy during the last half century.[4]

This variability has led many parts of the industry to reduce unneeded equipment and staff that could push them into bankruptcy should the economy slow. For example, at many homebuilding firms, payroll has been reduced to the minimum needed for administrative and project management purposes with the bulk of construction work subcontracted project by project or even day by day.[5] As a result, homebuilders increasingly manage the construction process rather than build homes themselves.

However, in seeking to minimize costs, the industry has reduced its ability to use innovations that require equipment or training, especially if either is expensive. This is because by shifting employees to trade contractors, all but the largest homebuilders lost the ability to influence the market for skilled and unskilled labor. Thus, builders no longer have the option to train their own workers to use innovations. Rather, they now need to find trade contractors with workers who have such training (or invest in it themselves). However, trade contractors also have reservations because of their own need to remain competitive and survive industry cycles. In addition, employee turnover is high in the construction trades, so there is little incentive for an employer to invest in training. Both homebuilders and trade contractors have therefore become risk-averse to training, which can lock them into using standard materials and procedures because the labor system is generally unable to provide anything more.

The Majority of Single-Family Homes Are Built by Small and Medium-Size Homebuilders

In 1997, there were about 470,000 single-family homebuilding firms in the United States.[6] These firms ranged from sole proprietorships

---

[4]Data from the U.S. Department of Commerce (2002) show that the three-year annual rolling "coefficient of variability" of fixed residential investment was 53 percent larger than the same measure of gross domestic product for the period 1946 to 1999.

[5]NAHB Research Center et al. (1989, p. 20).

[6]Data for firms with employees come from the U.S. Census Bureau (Table 5, 1999a; Table 5, 1999b; and Table 1, 2001a).

(i.e., a self-employed individual with no employees) to small, medium, and large firms. Of firms with employees, about one-third specialized in remodeling with the balance focused on building new homes.[7] However, because many sole proprietorships are believed to focus on remodeling, it is generally believed that remodelers represent more than one-third of all builders (see Figure 4.1).[8]

The most common type of homebuilding firm is the sole proprietorship, representing 70 percent. These firms typically coordinate the work of others or provide relatively narrow remodeling services. In 1997, these firms were responsible for 15 percent of the nation's annual residential construction work by dollar value.[9]

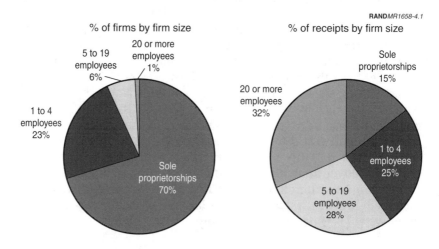

Figure 4.1—Single-Family Homebuilding Firms by Number of Employees
and by Annual Value of Residential Construction Put in Place, 1997

---

[7]U.S. Census Bureau (Table 10, 1999b).

[8]The regulatory reporting requirements for sole proprietorships vary by state. As a result, the business focus on sole proprietorships is not available for the country as a whole.

[9]Although sole proprietorships represent nearly 75 percent of the number of businesses in the United States, they typically represent only 3 percent of national receipts. The fact that sole proprietors represent 15 percent of receipts in the homebuilding industry demonstrates that they have a much larger effect than the national average. See www.census.gov/prod/www/abs/nonemp.html.

Small homebuilders having one to four employees were the second-largest category of homebuilder. These firms represented 23 percent of homebuilders and they completed 25 percent of 1997 residential construction work by dollar value.

Medium-sized homebuilders having between five and 19 employees represented 6 percent of firms and completed 28 percent of the value of residential construction. Finally, large homebuilders, sometimes also referred to as production builders, having 20 or more employees accounted for less than 1 percent of firms, but they put in place 32 percent of the value of the nation's residential construction activity.

These statistics show that although 32 percent of the nation's residential construction work is conducted by a few large firms, 68 percent is performed by firms with fewer than 20 employees. This means that the overwhelming majority of the nation's homes are built and remodeled by firms of modest size. However, even more important, almost 40 percent of the residential construction value is completed by firms with four or fewer employees. Finally, an astonishing 93 percent of homebuilding firms—or 435,000 firms—have four or fewer employees.

These characteristics reveal that small homebuilding firms have a very large effect on the nation's new and existing housing stock. For this reason, they play a large role in determining the rate of innovation in housing. Although the general literature on innovation argues that small companies are often more innovative than large ones, the competitive and cyclical nature of the industry usually means that these homebuilders have insufficient resources to learn about new innovations much less to invent or develop new ones of their own. In addition, because small homebuilders lack the economies of scale of larger builders, they are unlikely to adopt innovations unless they provide significant productivity gains.[10]

Others argue that the logistical difficulties inherent in communicating with small and medium-sized builders place large builders in a better position to promote innovation, since they arguably have more employees and capital, better access to information, and more influence with trade contractors. However, large builders counter

---

[10]NAHB Research Center et al. (1989, p. 19).

that they build homes so quickly that if they were to adopt an innovation shortly after its introduction, the innovation would already be widely deployed before any defects were identified. To support this argument, they cite past innovations such as fire-retardant treated plywood, "barrier-type" Exterior Insulation Finishing Systems (EIFSs), and polybutylene plumbing, which were widely deployed before problems appeared requiring replacement, sometimes at significant cost to homebuilders.[11]

Furthermore, since many of the largest builders are publicly held companies, these firms argue that adopting innovations before they are proven to be safe, reliable, and profitable violates their responsibility to shareholders and diminishes their standing with investment analysts who are wary of exposing themselves to unnecessary risks. As a result, large builders argue that it is better for small homebuilders with less at risk to experiment with and validate innovations first.

In short, despite the diversity inherent in homebuilding firms, builders of all sizes find reasons to be wary of innovations, often leading them to stay with the status quo.

Fragmentation Slows Information Sharing and Innovation Acceptance

Another defining characteristic of the housing industry is that it is fragmented along geographic, vertical, and horizontal dimensions. Geographic fragmentation results from municipal regulation, industry competitiveness, and the predominance of smaller builders. This type of fragmentation makes it more difficult for innovations to spread. Accordingly, an innovation may be accepted in one area of the country but not in another. In addition, because codes vary from place to place and firms tend to be small, many homebuilders work in only one or a few jurisdictions, thereby slowing the passage of information through informal networks.

---

[11]For a representative discussion of these problems, see NAHB Research Center (2001c).

The sheer number and small size of firms also result in horizontal fragmentation. Even within a geographic area, homebuilders may not directly communicate with most of their competitors, and trade contractors typically do not interact with other skilled trades to look for innovations that would improve their collective product or productivity.[12] An important countervailing force, however, is the high turnover rates in the homebuilding industry, which means that there is a relatively large flow of information among firms through the workers themselves. In addition, industry and association magazines, newsletters, advertisements, and web sites continue to improve the flow of innovation information, but educating all aspects of the industry still requires significant time and effort. Unfortunately, the high turnover of staff is likely to deter investment in training, and free flowing information over the Internet is not the same as training and experience.

Finally, the industry is also vertically fragmented, because most firms focus on a single stage of the homebuilding process rather than on several stages. As a result, firms operate independently and have few incentives to innovate in ways that might help others unless they were to capture benefits sufficiently large to justify the innovation on its own. The even larger challenge posed by vertical fragmentation, however, is that it complicates the sharing and disseminating of information, which, as Chapter Two showed, is a key factor in whether a decision agent decides to adopt an innovation. For example, a homebuyer may request that the builder use a new building material that he or she read about on the Internet. However, the builder may resist if the innovation's costs, benefits, or risks are unfamiliar; if trade contractors do not know how to install it; and if suppliers do not stock it. Finally, builders may also resist if they fear that code inspectors will not allow it.[13] A final manifestation of the negative effect of vertical fragmentation is that it makes it difficult for manufac-

---

[12]NAHB Research Center (1991, p. 23); and Slaughter (1993).

[13]Evaluation reports, as described in Chapter Three, are intended to address all of these concerns by stating under what conditions an innovation satisfies each of the model codes.

turers to obtain feedback from customers or builders about new product ideas.[14]

The net effect of fragmentation is that it increases the number of people who need to learn about an innovation and it decreases the efficiency with which they can learn about it. As a result, it lengthens the duration of the innovation process by requiring that more participants play the role of enabling, influence, and decision agents.[15]

Benefits of Innovations Are Often Hard to Protect

The housing industry, and the homebuilding process especially, are largely process-based. In almost all cases, the process is open and transparent to a large number of outside contractors. As a result, unlike high-tech industries such as electronics and biotechnology where innovators can protect their innovations through secrecy and patents, it is more difficult for homebuilders and others in the housing industry to protect their innovations.

In the case of product innovations, the scarce funds used to develop the innovation must also be used to register and protect the innovation's intellectual property. This is more than many firms can afford. In the case of process innovations (i.e., innovations that alter how a home is built), protecting them is difficult—especially for small and medium-size builders—because of their dependence on outside contractors who may take their ideas to other job sites.[16] Innovators may also resist seeking code approval or code modifications, since many of these processes occur in open, public forums potentially giving competitors the opportunity to introduce an imitation.[17]

---

[14]Construction industry studies have shown that many intermediate building product innovations are developed by builders and then communicated to the product manufacturers for commercialization and further development. Vertical fragmentation can undermine this process, as can innovations that span multiple firms. See Slaughter (1993).

[15]This conclusion is shared by innovation researchers. For example, von Hippel (1988) found that fragmentation in an industry deters innovation, because of the complex interactions among participants that may be required to introduce new products and methods.

[16]NAHB Research Center (1998, 2001b); and NAHB Research Center et al. (1989, p. ii).

[17]Dave Conover, National Evaluation Service, personal communication, July 12, 2002.

Each of these characteristics reduces the incentive for individuals and firms to promote innovation. Although the difficulty of protecting innovation means that low-cost, easily implemented innovations have few barriers to dissemination, it is far more important to realize that without incentives, innovations will not be created and there will be nothing to be diffused.

PARTICIPANTS MOTIVES TOWARD INNOVATION

Chapter Three showed how the industry's participants work together to put a homebuyer in a new home. That presentation may suggest that homebuilding is a relatively straightforward process, but in reality it is quite complex. Many complexities stem from the fact that building a single home requires that many thousands of decisions be made by hundreds of individuals.

Sometimes these decisions are made using the agent-based model described in Chapter Two. In other cases, decisions are made after negotiating with others or considering how others will respond to decisions with which they disagree. It is the aggregation of the many millions of decisions made throughout the industry each year that defines the status quo and creates opportunities for change and innovation.

In this section, we step through the homebuilding process and review the primary motives of participants and how those motives are likely to influence their inclination toward innovation.[18] This is important because, as Chapters Two and Three showed, throughout the homebuilding process, participants are routinely thrust into and rotate through the roles of *decision agent, enabling agent,* and *influence agent.*[19] For this reason, it is important to understand participants' motives and how they decide to support or not support an innovation.

---

[18]As explained in Chapter Three, this discussion will focus on the most directly involved participants, and each will be discussed only in the stage where they are most involved.

[19]Although it is tempting to think of the land developer as the decision agent in the land development stage, or the homebuilder in the construction stage, in reality many decisions must be negotiated with other parties such as designers, building departments, trade contractors, and lenders.

Before beginning this discussion, recall that the motives presented are the result of insights gathered during conversations with individuals from industry, government, and academia over the course of three years of research on housing innovation. By sharing these insights, we seek to illuminate why groups are more or less likely to support an innovation by putting innovation in the context of their primary responsibilities and functions. We would have preferred to use quantitative behavioral data describing what participants do rather than what they say, but such data are not available and collecting them would have been beyond the scope of this study. Accordingly, the reader should recognize that the motives presented will not necessarily represent all participants. (This would also be true of quantitative data had they been available.) In short, the reader should use this discussion to gain general insight into each group and how they may view innovation in general.

Last, to provide greater insight into housing innovations themselves, each section of this chapter also presents several examples of innovations that are in various stages of development and deployment. These examples help to illustrate both the benefits and the challenges to innovation.

Land Development

Innovations in the land development stage are mostly, but not entirely, land-use innovations. Although land-use innovations may seem unrelated to the homes ultimately built on that land, the decisions made in this stage often have much larger effects on homes than those that occur later in the homebuilding process. This is because lot size, orientation, and proximity to open space, neighbors, and transportation corridors can all affect the type and characteristics of the final home. In addition, land-use innovations may have significantly larger effects on residents' quality of life, the environment, and society than almost any other innovation. Once made, these decisions are largely irreversible.

Several examples of land development innovations include the following:

- *Designing Lots for Solar Access.* Orienting individual lots with their long axis running east to west maximizes access to solar energy (i.e., it maximizes the southern exposure). This allows the architect to harness the sun's energy to heat the home in the winter while using roof overhangs to shade the home in the summer. This simple step can save significant energy and money over the life of the home.[20]

- *Planning for Smart Growth.* Meeting housing demand by planning for higher density, mixed use, open space, transit, and walking access can increase the quality of life for residents and help protect the environment.

- *Information Technology for Land Development.* An innovation unrelated to land use is for local governments to use information technology and the Internet to provide faster, more accurate, and more complete access to information about publicly available land and property records such as land-use plans, zoning status, tax records, maps, covenants, and proffers among much else.[21]

Developers. The principal business of land developers is to buy undeveloped land, to prepare it for resale, and then to sell it. Since all money, whether borrowed or not, has a time value, developers have a strong motivation to complete the land development process as quickly as possible.

This emphasis on speed challenges the innovation process in five ways. First, developers need time to learn about an innovation. Second, if they want to adopt it, they need to find land development designers and contractors who are qualified and willing to do such work. Third, if an innovation requires rezoning the land (i.e., changing zoning from single family to mixed use), the developer must make the case before the local planning and zoning department. Similarly, if an innovation requires a change in an existing restrictive covenant, it may be too time consuming or expensive to obtain a waiver. Finally, depending on the nature of the innovation, the developer may need to convince investors that the innovation is likely to benefit them as well.

---

[20]For more information, see North Carolina Solar Center (2002). Another useful reference is the U.S. Department of Energy (2002d).

[21]One example is the Land Development System (LDSnet) of Fairfax County, Virginia, Department of Planning and Zoning. See Virginia Department of Planning and Zoning (n.d.).

This last concern is particularly important, because some land-use innovations may be perceived as reducing the value of the land, because changes may increase design and development costs, reduce the number of lots for sale, and potentially reduce the sales price of individual lots. For these reasons, developers (as well as their investors) may consider land-use innovations too risky—at least until others have demonstrated that they can be applied profitably.

Planning and Zoning Departments and Elected Officials. A developer may need to obtain approvals from planning and zoning departments or elected officials or both to start a development consistent with existing zoning, depending on local laws. However, if a developer also seeks to change the current zoning, a more extensive process including public hearings may be required.

Since these bodies operate in public view, including through public hearings, land-use decisions often attract significant community interest and public comment. These efforts may add cost and delay to the development process. Therefore, developers may avoid or minimize such requests if they believe the change or proposed innovation would not be broadly supported by the community or would not lead to a net reduction in cost or time.[22] This can potentially reduce the use of such innovations.

Community Interest Groups. Community interest groups often seek to influence major projects and land-use decisions. They do this by lobbying local officials, speaking at public hearings, advertising in the print or television media, or directly engaging the public. Depending on their specific cause and whether an innovation helps or hurts that cause, they may take a strong position either for or against an innovation. These groups may seek to preserve the status quo as a way to protect the property values of their own existing homes among other social causes. In many cases, in preserving the status quo these groups oppose innovations that are conspicuous or might otherwise change the character of the community.

---

[22]Some innovations may reduce the construction time or cost on their own, but related public input may reduce these benefits. As a result, developers generally consider the net benefits when deciding whether to adopt an innovation.

Design

Design stage innovations grow the knowledge base used to improve the products and processes that shape a home. Since knowledge is used by all participants, design innovations are exceptionally broad. Examples of design innovations include the following:

- *Computer-Based Design Tools.* Energy-10 and DOE-2 help designers increase a home's energy efficiency by using systems analysis to optimize window size and placement, roof overhangs, and air-conditioning sizing among other things.[23]

- *Information Dissemination via the Internet.* The Internet is also transforming how information reaches designers because manufacturers can now share information directly and efficiently via the web. This is providing architects, engineers, and especially homebuyers with more information to shape the design of the home.[24]

- *Advances in Building Materials and Products.* Design innovations can also improve building materials, products, and processes. For example, I-joists, pre-cast foundations, and insulating concrete forms (ICFs) show how new designs can lead to innovative building materials and products.[25]

Architects and Engineers. Although architects and engineers often see themselves as the primary sources of innovation, their professional obligations also require that they understand the cost and performance implications of innovations. This presents a challenge for innovations with which they are unfamiliar and for which little independent and objective information is available. In addition, residential architects and engineers generally have limited resources available to acquire information about innovations or to explain the merits of innovations to clients.

---

[23]For more information on these and other computer-based design tools, see www.eren.doe.gov/buildings/energy_tools/doe_tools.html. A recently completed assessment of the effect of the DOE-2 program can be found in National Research Council (2001, pp. 100–104).

[24]NAHB Research Center (2001b, pp. 33–34).

[25]These innovations are discussed in NAHB Research Center (2001c); and Phillips (2001, pp. 72–74).

The huge volume and relative simplicity of residential construction, as compared to commercial and industrial construction, lead to fewer, shorter, and generally more routine interactions. As a result, residential architects and engineers may avoid using innovations—especially innovations without evaluation reports—that they worry will be difficult to explain to those in the regulatory system.

Homebuyers. When looking to buy or build a home, homebuyers look for many things, but innovation is typically less important than are location, aesthetics, value, the chance for appreciation, and the quality of the neighborhood and surrounding schools.[26] For this reason, although homeowners are often interested in innovations that could improve energy efficiency, increase durability, or lower maintenance costs, this interest is typically mitigated if the innovation is perceived as potentially reducing other important traits such as the present or future value of the home.

Testing, Certification, and Evaluation Groups. Taken together, testing, certification, and evaluation groups play a critical role in enabling innovation. By providing a mechanism to independently, objectively, and professionally test, certify, and evaluate performance with respect to codes and standards, these groups and the reports they produce quickly and credibly provide the information needed by designers, builders, and code officials. Also, by freely distributing evaluation reports on the Internet, the housing industry will increasingly have instantaneous access (including through wireless access) to these important documents.

Pre-Construction

Innovations relevant to the pre-construction phase include those that change how plans are reviewed, permits issued, and building materials produced among others. Examples of these types of innovations include the following:

- *Internet Tools for Regulation, Management, and Information Sharing.* Information technology (IT) can be used to streamline the pre-construction phase. Although still in the early phases of

---

[26]Sweaney et al. (2001).

adoption, moving portions of the plan review permitting processes onto the web can increase speed and convenience while lowering costs. IT can also be used to share code changes and product evaluations more quickly, potentially even in the field using wireless technology. Management tools can help builders schedule subcontractors and material procurement while helping material producers and product manufacturers better manage their supply chains.[27]

- *Manufacturing Advances.* New processes for manufacturing materials, products, and components can also improve the preconstruction phase. For example, improving the efficiency and automating the production of pre-fabricated components (e.g., roof trusses and wall sections) or even building housing in development-specific assembly lines are important innovations.[28]

Model Code Organizations. The membership of model code groups generally consists of public code officials and the private sector. During the course of any given year, technical committees hold hearings and prepare proposals for consideration at the code group's annual meeting. The technical committees consist of industry personnel and public safety officials, but most model codes are changed only if a majority of public safety officials nominated by their state and local governments vote in favor of a committee proposal. Although many feel that a system of "democratic voting by public officials" is the best decision process for ensuring that the public interest is served, others argue that it slows the rate at which the codes change and innovations can be introduced.[29]

Regulatory Agencies. In seeking to enforce existing building codes, regulatory officials sometimes prefer conventional designs, materials, and products to innovations since they are already familiar with

---

[27]More detailed discussions of these innovations can be found in NAHB Research Center (2001b); and Hassell et al. (2000). In addition, the National Conference of States on Building Codes and Standards has significant information on these issues on its web site at www.ncsbcs.org/.

[28]These innovations are discussed in NAHB Research Center (2001a); and Phillips (2001, pp. 72–74).

[29]The voting and larger decision processes used by model code groups is a heated topic. Interested readers should visit the web sites of the International Code Council and the National Fire Protection Association to learn more about this debate.

them. However, when agency personnel consider innovations, they typically need more time to determine if they meet local requirements (possibly by reviewing the evaluation reports and other documentation). Depending on how long it takes for agency personnel to make this decision, the time or cost benefits of using the innovation may be diminished.[30]

Material Producers, Product Manufacturers, and Pre-Fabricators. The producers of building materials, products, and components seek to make a profit by selling quality products to broad and niche markets. To do this, they may consider a number of factors beyond the product itself.

Suppliers. Similarly, suppliers want to earn a profit by stocking the products and materials their customers want. Although suppliers do not oppose innovation, they may be less inclined to stock an innovation of which their customers are unaware.

Construction

Innovations in the construction stage change how homebuilders and trade contractors physically construct the home. In many cases, construction innovations are influenced by material, product, and component innovations that occur in the design and pre-construction stages. However, in other cases, innovations relate to information technology and construction-related process innovations. Sample construction innovations include the following:

- *Using IT to Streamline Field Inspections.* IT can be used to streamline the scheduling of field inspections as well as to aid with the inspections themselves and needed record-keeping and follow-up[31]

- *Pre-Fabricated Components and Alternative Materials.* Building homes from pre-fabricated components (e.g., pre-cast footers, wall panels, roof trusses) or alternative materials such as insulat-

---

[30]Field and Rivkin (1975).

[31]See NAHB Research Center (2001b); Hassell et al. (2000); and the web site of the National Conference of States on Building Codes and Standards at www.ncsbcs.org/.

ing concrete forms or steel framing can potentially speed construction while improving quality.

- *Improved Construction Techniques.* Better sealing around windows, improving fresh air ventilation, and placing heating, ventilating, and air-conditioning (HVAC) ducts in conditioned spaces can improve energy efficiency and reduce energy bills.

Homebuilders. Homebuilders stay in business by building quality homes at a profit. Therefore, builders are motivated to improve the coordination and productivity of trade contractors, reduce the cost of materials, and ensure that regulatory requirements are met. Acting on these motives requires evaluating changes in the price and quality of labor and materials, the potential for call-back repairs or liability, the long-term importance of goodwill and cooperation with trade contractors and suppliers, and weighing the regulatory and "market" risk of innovations that may not be familiar to field inspectors or desired by homeowners.

An additional dimension to builder motives and how builders weigh innovation-related decisions relates to the size of the building firms themselves. Small and medium-sized builders might intentionally use visible innovations such as high-performance windows and placing ducts in air-conditioning spaces to differentiate their homes. Large builders, however, may prefer "hidden" innovations such as pre-fabricated components that can improve productivity while still producing homes that look traditional. This is particularly true with larger housing developments where large builders can establish such techniques as the communitywide standard for how homes are built.

Trade Contractors. Trade contractors typically provide a narrow set of services defined by skills learned on the job or through special training. Since these services are largely defined by past experiences and often by the codes themselves, contractors may have few motivations to adopt an innovation. This is especially true if the innovation could reduce the demand for their services.

Finally, the skills and experiences amassed by skilled laborers can either help or hurt innovation. This is because their knowledge can either be combined with creativity to develop a new way of doing something, or their knowledge can constrain their creativity and cause them to simply accept traditional approaches without question. Several innovation researchers argue that creativity often leads to process innovations on the job site, but they often go unnoticed, since there are no mechanisms for recognizing or communicating these innovations to others.[32]

Post-Construction

After a home is built, there are many opportunities for innovation. But the true importance of innovation in the post-construction phase is that many decisions about innovation occurring earlier in the process are influenced by how designers and homebuilders anticipate that the parties in the post-construction stage will react to their decisions. Since successfully selling a home requires finding a buyer, arranging financing, and obtaining insurance, designers and builders consider how these parties will react to an innovation before they make a decision to use it. As a result, the post-construction phase is recognized as exerting significant indirect pressure on whether innovations are adopted in the earlier stages.[33] Examples of innovations that directly and indirectly affect the post-construction stage include the following:

- *Database on the Effect of Innovations on Real Estate Prices.* Databases that store and share information on the market value of innovations can help appraisers, Realtors, homeowners, and homebuilders learn about how innovations are valued by the real estate market.[34]

- *Mortgage Underwriting Software.* In the mid-1990s, Freddie Mac and Fannie Mae each introduced mortgage underwriting software to standardize and accelerate loan evaluation, issuance, and transferring the mortgage to the secondary market. This

---

[32]Slaughter (1993).

[33]Personal communication during an industry roundtable discussion on "Housing Innovation and the Appraisal Process," organized by NAHB Research Center, Bowie, Md., December 18, 2001.

[34]One example is the Appraisal Institute Residential Database that seeks to provide a nationwide source of appraisal data, including innovative homes. However, its potential will be realized only if the database is populated, easily accessible, and broadly used. For more information on this effort, see www.airdport.com/. Also see Harney (2000, p. G01).

software has helped the nation's 25,000 mortgage brokers increase the percentage of mortgages they originate from 20 percent in the early 1990s to more than 50 percent by 2000.[35]

- *Innovation-Promoting Mortgages.* Several secondary lenders offer mortgages that reward housing innovations such as energy efficiency, renewable energy, sustainable or "green" materials, or access to public transit.[36] These mortgages use the estimated cost savings from reduced energy and transportation costs to either increase the size of the loan or improve its terms.[37]

- *Analysis and Dissemination of the Benefits of Innovations to Insurers.* Once quantitative information on the performance of innovations is available, analysis and dissemination of results help insurers, lenders, Realtors, and homeowners better understand the potential risk-reducing benefits of some innovations.[38]

- *Computer-Based Remodeling Tools.* Homeowners can also benefit from computer-based tools that help them learn how to remodel their homes in ways that can save them money and increase its value. Although many product manufacturers and their associations offer tools to better quantify the benefits of their products (e.g., washing machines, windows), state and federal agencies do so as well.[39]

---

[35]In exchange for a small fee, mortgage brokers can evaluate loans and sell them directly to the secondary market without partnering with a bank and other traditional lenders. For more information see Freddie Mac (1996); and Barta (2001).

[36]See Fannie Mae (2002).

[37]See Spring 2001 *PATHways* Newsletter at www.pathnet.org/pathways/pw_spr01.pdf or the U.S. Department of Energy (2002e).

[38]The "Fortified Home" program of the insurance industry's Institute for Business and Home Safety (IBHS) provides participating insurers with guidelines on safety features relevant to hazards in a given geographic area. These guidelines can then be used to offer discounted premiums or deductible waivers to homebuyers who buy homes that have these features. See PATH Working Group on Barriers/Insurance (1999).

[39]One user-friendly tool focused on energy savings is the Home Energy Saver developed and maintained by the Department of Energy's Lawrence Berkeley National Laboratory; see homeenergysaver.lbl.gov (accessed June 8, 2002). Another tool focused on durability is the National Economic Service-Life Tool (NEST). This tool will inform homeowners and homebuilders about how building material selection can improve durability and lower long-term maintenance costs.

Real Estate Agents and Salespersons. Real estate agents and salespersons seek to match buyers, sellers, and homes. When it comes to homes with innovations, their ability to fulfill this role depends on whether they are aware of those innovations, their costs and benefits, and how they affect the perceived value of the home to those who do and do not value the innovation. Thus, agents or salespersons need to be fairly knowledgeable about an innovation and its positive or negative aspects. This possibly difficult level of awareness must be accomplished before innovations can become common.

Mortgage Brokers. To match homebuyers and lenders, mortgage brokers estimate the borrower's ability to pay, work with an appraiser to estimate the home's value, and seek financing from a lender. In general, their motives are to complete the entire process quickly and easily while not overestimating the value of a home, since the lender may review this closely. A broker may therefore prefer to use a standard appraisal, rather than a custom appraisal, which may cause a home with innovations to be more conservatively valued. The desire to complete the process quickly and easily may also lead the broker to prefer using standard mortgages rather than innovative mortgages such as those focused on energy efficiency, which may require or be perceived as requiring specialized training, processing time, and costs.

Appraisers. In estimating the market value of a home, appraisers may moderate their valuation so as to neither overestimate nor underestimate its value. This helps ensure that banks do not make a larger loan than could be recovered if the borrower defaults. However, in seeking to moderate the appraisal, they may tend toward local averages alone rather than taking into account the effect that an innovation may have on that average. This is because appraisers, especially those conducting a standard appraisal, may not have the necessary information to accurately value it. Unless they are being paid for a custom appraisal, appraisers are unlikely to have the time or resources to investigate how and if an innovation should affect the value of the home. As a result, although appraisers play a critical role in recognizing and certifying the value of an innovation, they do not have strong incentives to learn about them.[40]

---

[40]For a detailed discussion of the these issues, see NAHB Research Center (2002).

Primary and Secondary Lenders. Fundamentally, primary and secondary lenders want to make sure that a borrower has sufficient credit and income so as to not default on a loan. In addition, they want to make sure that the home is not overvalued so that, regardless of who holds the mortgage, the value of the loan can be recovered if the borrower defaults.

From this point on, the motivations of lenders begin to differ, especially as related to innovations, because, although innovations can affect a home's market value, they can also make homes more affordable. Since some primary and secondary lenders are public corporations or quasi-government institutions, they typically have a special obligation to making homes more affordable. This means that innovations that reduce energy costs, maintenance costs, insurance risks, or transportation costs all provide a way to help fulfill this public charge. For this reason, lenders with public ties, and in the long run all lenders, have an incentive to recognize and adjust loan terms because of the presence of a beneficial innovation. However, because few innovations have sufficient data available on either their performance and ability to reduce costs or their effect on default rates, these innovative mortgage products are still rarely used.

Insurers. In measuring risk and setting insurance rates, insurers seek to quantitatively determine how an individual home is likely to compare to others. Since most homes use similar materials, products, and methods, insurers have a wealth of data on how they perform under extreme conditions such as wind, flood, fire, and snow. However, innovations suffer from a lack of data about how they perform (e.g., how does a new structural systems endure high wind, how does a new roofing system resist fire).

Many of the methods insurers use to analyze and manage risk cannot easily be applied to innovations. When insurers are unsure how to measure and manage risks posed by an innovation, they do not know whether to award a discount based on a lower risk, charge a higher premium for a higher risk (or increased uncertainty), or simply reject the applicant.[41] As a result, insurers and those anticipating their re-

---

[41]PATH Working Group on Barriers/Insurance (1999).

action to innovations may choose not to adopt innovations, thereby contributing to slowing the rate of innovation in housing.

IMPLICATIONS FOR INNOVATION

This chapter has shown that although innovations continue to occur, industry characteristics and participant motives often present additional challenges to innovations. For example, low barriers to entry, cyclical business cycles, and the predominance of small firms tend to reduce the willingness of builders to try innovations. Fragmentation and the difficulty of protecting innovations also increase the cost and risk of completing the innovation process. Furthermore, since the primary responsibilities of many industry participants are defined by issues other than innovation, increasing their awareness of innovations is quite challenging.

As stated in this chapter's opening, many of the insights described have been informed by the authors' discussions with industry participants over several years. As also stated in the opening, the reader should recognize that what people say is often different from what they do. Since quantitative behavioral data were not readily available and since gathering such data was beyond the scope of this study, the strongest conclusion this chapter can draw is that the structural aspects of the industry and the primary motives of its participants are likely to slow the rate of innovation. As a result, the benefits that innovation can provide are realized more slowly than they otherwise might be.

This conclusion leads to the following question: If the housing industry innovates more slowly than we would like, what can be done to increase the rate of innovation? As a first step to answering this question, the next chapter reviews past efforts by the federal government to do just that.

Chapter Five

FEDERAL EFFORTS TO PROMOTE INNOVATION IN HOUSING

EVOLUTION OF THE FEDERAL APPROACH TO INNOVATION

The federal government has long recognized the importance of innovation, although the specific reasons and strategies for supporting it have evolved over time. The modern era of federal support for innovation began during World War II when, in the interests of national security, the federal government supported the development of radar and nuclear weapons. Later, during the energy crises of the 1970s, rising costs and concerns about declining supplies of fossil fuel led the government to support innovation in fossil fuel production, renewable energy, and energy efficiency. Still later, the government began to focus on promoting innovation in the health sciences to prolong and improve quality of life. Beyond these specific critical areas, the government has also promoted innovation in other industries because of its ability to increase productivity and boost prosperity and living standards.[1] Promoting innovation has now emerged as a major strategy for boosting economic growth and improving quality of life.

Just as the reasons for promoting innovation have evolved, so too have the strategies for pursuing it. Most notably, the strategies have shifted from supporting just one aspect of the innovation process

---

[1]Council of Economic Advisors (2000, p. 97).

(for example, basic or exploratory research) to supporting many of its aspects as described in Chapter Two. These changes reflect an evolution toward a more sophisticated understanding of the subtle challenges involved in promoting innovation. This evolution reflects an implicit recognition that narrow efforts are unlikely to succeed on their own and that multiple efforts need to work in harmony to leverage each other in a more systematic approach.

This chapter presents and briefly discusses a number of federal efforts to promote innovation in housing.[2] The purpose is not to evaluate these efforts per se but rather to identify them, explain their strategies, and discuss their effect on the innovation process.

To help put the housing industry and federal efforts to promote housing innovation in context, this chapter begins by reviewing the federal government's general efforts to promote innovation throughout the entire economy. After this introduction, a more specific discussion of housing efforts will follow.

BROAD-BASED FEDERAL EFFORTS TO PROMOTE INNOVATION

Before World War II, most federal efforts to promote innovation were small and focused on specific public goods such as vaccine development, reducing topsoil erosion, and controlling agricultural pests.[3] Upon entering World War II, federal spending on innovation increased sharply but fell once the war ended, since R&D was not considered to be a major government responsibility. However, the Cold War, the Korean War, and particularly the Soviet launch of the Sputnik satellite in 1957 ultimately changed this view. Following these events, federal R&D spending increased rapidly and the nation's capacity in science and technology came to be seen as an important foundation for ensuring national security.[4]

---

[2]This is not an exhaustive review but rather a representative sample of past efforts to promote innovation in housing.

[3]Ruttan (2001).

[4]Blanpied (2000).

Government thinking toward the federal role in R&D and innovation further expanded in the 1980s. Executive and legislative leadership put a high priority on strengthening the national technology and innovation system. Science and technology came to be seen as critical to both national security *and* national economic competitiveness as well as quality of life.[5] Moreover, government, industry, and academia recognized that although industry had shown a remarkable ability to create new technologies and innovate, there were market failures, information barriers, and externalities beyond the purview of private enterprises to address. As a result, a consensus emerged that the government had a responsibility to increase the provision of public goods not adequately provided by private markets (e.g., basic or high-risk research) as well as to limit externalities that resulted from certain private-sector actions (e.g., environmental pollution).

Federal Support of Research and Development

Since World War II, federal investment in R&D has steadily grown; in 2002 the federal investment in unclassified R&D stood at roughly $100 billion. In general, these efforts were intended to contribute to the foundation of scientific knowledge. Accordingly, results were published in publicly available, peer-reviewed journals even though the results often belonged to the government. This approach was generally considered successful, since public and private investments in R&D were often complementary. For example, federal R&D funds frequently concentrated on basic research where risks were high, market funding not available, or federal investment might produce potential future high payoffs for society. This is in comparison to industry-funded R&D that generally focused on development and commercialization.[6]

---

[5]U.S. House of Representatives (1998); and U.S. General Accounting Office (1997).

[6]During the 1990s, industry R&D became increasingly focused on short-term R&D. According to the Industrial Research Institute, 70 percent of industry R&D investments were focused on projects potentially providing near-term gains, 7 percent went to basic research, and the balance went to applied research. See Larson (2002).

Expanding Support for Innovation Beyond R&D

In the 1980s, low productivity growth in the United States was believed to be a key reason why the U.S. economy was falling behind that of countries such as Japan.[7] Partly in response, the federal government expanded its support of innovation beyond the funding of R&D. These efforts included the following:

- The Bayh-Dole Patent and Trademark Act of 1980 allowed the performers of federally funded research to apply for patents and obtain exclusive licenses on research results. This encouraged universities, small businesses, and private industry to invest in developing and commercializing inventions supported by public dollars.[8]

- The Stevenson-Wydler Technology Innovation Act of 1980 approved the transfer (i.e., licensing) of technologies developed at public research laboratories to states, localities, and industry.

- In 1986, the Stevenson-Wydler Act was amended to allow for Cooperative Research and Development Agreements (CRADAs) that authorized federal laboratories to work with private firms and universities to develop inventions for commercial application.

Together, these and other pieces of legislation made it easier for individuals and firms to invest in, develop, and protect innovations, especially when innovations were partially or fully sponsored by government. However, even these improvements did not lead to a streamlined innovation process.

Systematic Efforts to Promote the Innovation Process

Through the sponsorship of R&D and the passage of legislation, federal agencies have launched programs to promote innovation when

---

[7] U.S. House of Representatives (1998); and U.S. General Accounting Office (1997).

[8] More fully, the Bayh-Dole Act allows federal agencies to grant exclusive patent licenses to private businesses, but the government retains a nonexclusive license to use the invention and it retains "march-in" rights where the funding agency can require the grantee, contractor, or licensee to grant a license on reasonable terms to a responsible applicant. See the Technology Transfer Legislation Summary at intramural.nimh.nih.gov/techtran/legislation.htm.

doing so could help advance their mission and goals. These programs often sought to provide a more systematic and tailored approach to promoting innovation. For example, rather than funding R&D alone, some agencies launched programs that helped explore new concepts; disseminate information about technology and standards; and help link scientists, engineers, and other innovators through conferences and exchanges. In short, these programs pursued innovation because it was a "means to an end."

Moreover, public-private partnerships emerged to coordinate and leverage the respective strengths and resources of the public, private, educational, and nonprofit sectors.[9] In most cases, the federal government still supports basic, high-risk research, but it is increasingly common to provide cost-shared funding and technical assistance for development and demonstration activities. In most cases, industry partners remain responsible for funding the commercial development of technologies and innovations that emerge from these partnerships. Examples of these federal efforts include the following:

- The Advanced Technology Program (ATP) of the National Institute of Standards and Technology (NIST) funds high-risk innovation projects.

- The Manufacturing Extension Program (MEP), also of NIST, helps firms solve business and technical problems through a nationwide network of Manufacturing Extension Centers and manufacturing experts.

- The Industries of the Future (IOF) program of DOE promotes collaborative R&D partnerships for energy-intensive industries (e.g., mining, metal casting, forest products, steel) to develop new and more efficient ways to use energy.[10]

- FreedomCAR, a public-private partnership between DOE and the nation's automobile manufacturers was launched in 2002. Building on the work of the earlier Partnership for a New Generation of Vehicles, this partnership's long-term goal is to per-

---

[9]U.S. General Accounting Office (1997).

[10]See the Industries of the Future home page at www.oit.doe.gov/industries.shtml, accessed July 15, 2002.

form high-risk research to develop technologies for hydrogen-powered fuel cell vehicles.[11]

To differing degrees, these programs have created formal and informal linkages across the innovation process in the hopes of improving communication and increasing the rate of innovation. Many regard these efforts as having contributed to increasing the rate of innovation beyond what industry would have performed on its own.

TARGETED FEDERAL EFFORTS TO PROMOTE INNOVATION IN HOUSING

As the nation struggled to define its interest in and approach to innovation in general, its efforts at promoting innovation in housing also evolved. These efforts began with direct federal funding of R&D, but they soon expanded to address other portions of the innovation process. Although the programs described in this section do not cover all that has been done or supported by the federal government, they provide a sense of the evolution in goals, scope, and strategy.

Federal Support of Housing R&D

As with the rest of the federal R&D portfolio, the portion related to housing is quite diverse, partly because housing R&D responds to a broad range of social needs and technical possibilities. For example, concerns about a housing shortage in the late 1960s led to research focused on mass production, and the energy crises of the 1970s led to a focus on energy efficiency and alternative energy research.[12]

The most recent assessment of housing R&D estimated that in fiscal year (FY) 1999, the federal government invested roughly $236 million in R&D potentially relevant to housing.[13] This represented only 0.6 percent of the entire 1999 federal nondefense R&D budget of roughly $40 billion.

---

[11]U.S. Department of Energy (2002a).

[12]According to Baer et al. (1976, pp. L1–L30), federal involvement in housing technology began as early as the 1940s.

[13]Hassell et al. (2001).

More important than the relative or absolute size of this investment, however, is its breadth and ability to lay a foundation of knowledge and invention to increase the rate of innovation. This breadth is illustrated in part by Figure 5.1, which organizes the federal investment into 15 categories. In addition, short descriptions of these categories and the estimated funding are provided in Table 5.1.

RAND*MR1658-5.1*

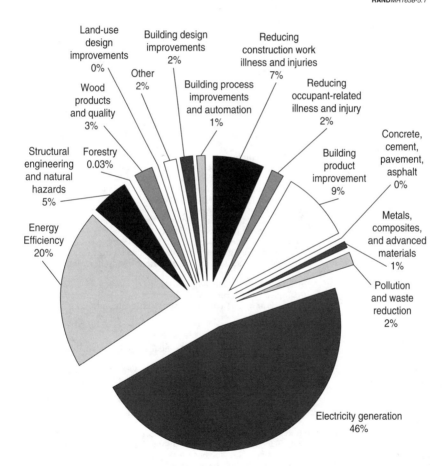

Figure 5.1—Federal FY 1999 Investments in Housing-Related R&D

Table 5.1

Overview of Federal FY 1999 Investments in Housing-Related R&D

R&D Category	Invest-ment ($ millions)	Sample Activities
Building design improvements	4.2	Improving residential design. Includes sustainable and green design, affordable housing, and improved building rehabilitation/renovation.
Building process improvements and automation	3.1	Improving the homebuilding process. Includes traditional process improvements, IT, and how IT can be transferred to housing.
Building product improvement	21.0	Earmarking about $12 million for window-related research with balance to general R&D (nearly $6 million), insulation ($1 million), alternatives to stick framing ($1 million), foundations, insulation, paint, roofing, and windows.
Concrete, cement, pavement, as-phalt	0.6	Developing cement-wood composite materials.
Energy efficiency	49.5	Spending $28 million on building energy systems, building codes and standards, existing buildings, heat and moisture modeling, and weatherization; $16 million on HVAC, appliances, and motors; $5 million for lighting.
Electricity generation	111.0	Spending more than $100 million on renewable energy including photovoltaics ($90 million), general solar and solar thermal ($6 million), and geothermal ($8 million); and an additional $7 million for building-related fuel cells.
Forestry	0.0078	Studying the effect of housing-related demand on wood markets; economic analysis of conservation tradeoffs; effect of forest and riparian forest buffers on residential development.
Land-use design improvements	0.3	Studying urban demolition, deconstruction, and redevelopment; the effect of natural resource conservation on rural subdivision development, sustainable development, and transportation issues.
Metals, composites, and advanced materials (not wood or con-crete)	1.9	Investing in metals and composites R&D including thermoplastic composites for structural applications, steel applications, and analysis of hybrid/composite structural walls and steel frame systems.
Other	3.7	Investing in multicategory R&D and dissemination and outreach of R&D results.
Pollution and waste reduction	3.9	Investing in refrigerant R&D ($2 million); wood processing ($1.7 million), and studying water and multipollutant issues.
Reducing construction work illness and injuries	15.9	Researching ways to reduce residential housing-construction-related illness and injuries (other portions of the occupational safety R&D likely to yield spillover benefits to housing).
Reducing occu-pant-related ill-ness and injury	4.2	Studying general indoor air quality ($3.1 million), $600,000 of which focused exclusively on residential air quality; sensor development; low solvent adhesives.
Structural engineering and natural hazards	11.5	Investing in multiple hazards R&D ($6 million); fire research ($3.7 million); earthquake and wind-related R&D (nearly $1 million each); smaller investments in structural R&D, measurement, and instrumentation.

Table 5.1—continued

R&D Category	Invest-ment ($ millions)	Sample Activities
Wood products and quality	5.9	Identifying new applications for wood and wood scrap/waste ($2.7 million); characterizing the structural properties of wood, wood structures, and adhesives ($1 million); smaller investments in wood-containing composites, wood drying, and wood preservatives.

Additional Support for Housing Innovation

As with broader federal efforts, funding R&D alone did not lead to the widespread deployment of new housing technologies. However, perhaps unlike other industries, housing was recognized early on as requiring more than just R&D to promote innovation. This is clearly demonstrated in the language of "Title V-Research and Technology" of the Housing and Urban Development Act of 1970 that explicitly stated:

> The Secretary shall require, to the greatest extent feasible, *the em-ployment of new and improved technologies, methods, and materials* in housing construction, rehabilitation, and maintenance under programs administered by him with a view to reducing costs, *and shall encourage and promote the acceptance and application of such advanced technology, methods, and materials* by all segments of the housing industry, communities, industries, engaged in urban de-velopment activities, and the general public.[14]

Thus, almost from the start of the federal role in housing innovation, it was realized that promoting innovation required more than simply funding R&D. To better shed light on the additional measures that have been used to support parts of the innovation process beyond R&D, several energy-related examples are identified and described below.

State Energy Codes. California implemented the first detailed, statewide energy code in 1975 to moderate growth in energy con-

---

[14]U.S. Congress (1970).

sumption.[15] Pushed by rising energy prices and the development of energy-related model codes, state energy codes soon followed. They spread even further in the mid-1990s when federal law required that each state consider revising its residential energy code to meet or exceed the 1992 Model Energy Code. Over the past 25 years, energy codes have varied in approach, stringency, and enforcement leading some to be more effective than others.[16] That said, energy codes are yet another tool for boosting innovation in building materials and construction methods.

Appliance Standards. In the late 1970s, individual states began to issue their own appliance efficiency standards. As this trend continued, national manufacturers came to support the creation of a federal program to set appliance standards that would preempt state standards. This led to the 1987 passage of the National Appliance Energy Conservation Act requiring that DOE issue and periodically revise minimum energy efficiency standards for the most energy-intensive household appliances. As of 2000, DOE estimated that these standards saved consumers a total of $28 billion (1999 dollars) in energy costs.[17] Although such estimates are fraught with difficulty, a recent study by the National Research Council (2001) found that improvements in refrigerator energy efficiency—driven by the technology push of federal R&D and the technology pull of appliance standards—reduced average refrigerator energy consumption by two-thirds since 1974 thereby reducing consumer electricity costs by $7 billion between 1981 and 1990 alone.

Energy Efficiency Mortgages. In 1979, a Presidential Executive Order directed federally sponsored secondary lenders to offer consumers incentives to purchase energy-efficient homes. This led to the creation of energy efficiency mortgages (EEMs), which traditionally increased the amount one could borrow. Today, EEMs continue to be offered by federally affiliated secondary lenders and several private lenders, but, as from the day they were initiated, they remain more

---

[15]See the state of California's entry in the U.S. Department of Energy's State Energy Codes database at www.energycodes.gov/implement/state_codes/index.stm, accessed July 15, 2002.

[16]For a discussion and analysis of the efficacy of state building codes, see Ortiz and Bernstein (1999).

[17]Federal Trade Commission (2002).

complex to obtain. For example, as of 1998, almost 20 years after EEMs were first introduced, only 1.5 percent of the loans made by a major federal lender were EEMs.[18]

Systematic Efforts to Support and Accelerate Innovation in Housing

In the case of housing, the government has long recognized that systematic efforts were needed rather than a set of narrow measures. This understanding was reflected by national and presidential commissions that were formed after the civil unrest of the mid-1960s to investigate the problems facing the nation's cities and urban housing in particular.[19] As a result of these commissions and their focus on industry characteristics that limited the production of housing, innovation was high on the national agenda, and significant pressure was placed on the new Secretary of the Department of Housing and Urban Development (itself created in 1965) to use technology to meet the nation's housing needs.

Operation Breakthrough. In response to congressional pressure and legislation, HUD announced Operation Breakthrough in 1969. Breakthrough was presented as a "partnership of labor, consumers, private enterprise, local, state, and federal government which would seek to provide housing for all income levels through the use of modern techniques of production, marketing, and management."[20]

This $72 million research and technology development program sought to industrialize housing construction while also changing people's perceptions of manufactured housing. The main premise was that by replacing traditional, craft-based production processes with machines and precision manufacturing, mass-produced housing would be more consistent, higher quality, and more affordable.

Despite its good intentions, Operation Breakthrough is widely recognized as being unsuccessful at promoting both technical and institu-

---

[18]Farhar (2000).

[19]These included the Douglas Commission (1966) and the Kaiser Commission (1967). For additional background see Baer et al. (1976, p. L1).

[20]Baer et al. (1976, p. L6).

tional change. Of the many analyses of Breakthrough's failures, perhaps the most enduring is that Operation Breakthrough's top-down, federal approach was incompatible with the locally regulated and highly fragmented housing industry.[21] In the words of a 1976 RAND study, Operation Breakthrough's

> multi-faceted approach to increased efficiency [was] several orders of magnitude more complex than simply funding R&D projects. . . . [T]he complexity [was] due to the need to cut at the problem from both sides of the market . . . in ways that involve several levels of government responsibility and bureaucracy [and for which] the available policy levers . . . [existed] at the state and local level.

Thus, an important aspect of Operation Breakthrough's downfall was that it sought to restructure the industry even though the federal government had very limited abilities to do so.

Advanced Housing Technology Program. In 1989, several years after the launch of DOE's appliance standards program, DOE expanded its work on innovation in housing by helping create the Advanced Housing Technology Program (AHTP). Formed as a public-private partnership involving DOE, the National Association of Home Builders, and the NAHB Research Center, AHTP sought to identify new and emerging technologies that could cost-effectively improve the energy efficiency and quality of homes, and to develop plans to promote and accelerate the adoption of the best innovations.

In working to accomplish these goals, AHTP prepared a historical record of innovation in home building, including an inventory of 40 years of housing innovations,[22] as well as studies on how innovations are diffused in homebuilding and how emerging technologies can be assessed to anticipate their likelihood of adoption.[23] After these efforts, AHTP proposed six strategies to accelerate the development and diffusion of innovations. These included improving communication and the assessment of market needs, sharing the costs of technology development and commercialization, reducing the risk to

---

[21]O'Brien et al. (2000).

[22]NAHB Research Center (1989a).

[23]NAHB Research Center et al. (1989); and NAHB Research Center (1989b).

buyers, and communicating the value of innovation throughout the industry.[24]

EnergyStar®. The Environmental Protection Agency introduced the EnergyStar label in 1992 as a voluntary labeling program to identify and promote the most energy-efficient products offered by manufacturers. The idea was to help recognize and promote manufacturers and products that could provide "the same or better performance as comparable models" while using less energy, saving money, and reducing pollution and the risk of climate change.

Beginning with computers and monitors, EnergyStar expanded into other types of office equipment and residential HVAC equipment. In 1996, EPA partnered with DOE to expand coverage of particular product categories. Today, EnergyStar evaluates and labels 30 product categories, including building materials (e.g., lighting, windows, and roofing products) and buildings themselves (e.g., homes, office buildings, schools, supermarkets, stores).[25]

In addition, EnergyStar created easy-to-use tools and technical information for both owners and designers to help them lower energy bills in both new and existing residential and commercial buildings. Available on the Internet, these tools include store locators to find EnergyStar products, electronic directories for information and help, and web-based diagnostic tools to help remodel and design all types of buildings.[26]

By simplifying the terminology and reducing the effort involved in defining and validating these improvements, EnergyStar has made it easier for individuals, firms, and the government to understand what the label means. As testament to the resulting simplicity, several national lenders have begun to offer EnergyStar mortgages, and the U.S. Army and Navy updated their housing procurement specifications in June 2000 to comply with the EnergyStar qualifications for new homes. Finally, EPA estimates that since EnergyStar's inception, 630 million products with its label have been sold, saving $5 billion in

---

[24]NAHB Research Center (1991).

[25]For a home to qualify for the EnergyStar label, it must be at least 30 percent more efficient than one built under the Model Energy Code.

[26]For example, see the Home Improvement Toolbox at www.epa.gov/hhiptool/.

energy costs in 2001 and reducing pollution without reducing product quality or functionality.[27]

The National Construction Goals and the Residential Implementation Plan. In the mid-1990s, the federal government's National Science and Technology Council (NSTC)[28] formed a subcommittee on construction and building to coordinate and focus the work of 14 federal agencies in enhancing the competitiveness of the U.S. construction industry and improve public and worker safety and environmental quality through research and development. In fulfilling its charge, the subcommittee was instructed to cooperate with U.S. industry, labor, and academia.[29]

Shortly thereafter, the subcommittee studied research priorities expressed by the construction industry in industry forums and in proposals submitted to the Department of Commerce's ATP. After reviewing these materials, the subcommittee proposed seven goals for research, development, and demonstration for general use by the construction industry.[30] After further discussion and backing by industry leaders, the following were presented as National Construction Goals:

- 50 percent reduction in project delivery times,

- 50 percent reduction in operations, maintenance, and energy costs,

- 30 percent increase in occupant productivity and comfort,

- 50 percent fewer facility-related illnesses and injuries,

- 50 percent less waste and pollution,

- 50 percent greater durability and flexibility, and

- 50 percent reduction in construction illnesses and injuries.

---

[27]See fact sheet at www.epa.gov/nrgystar/newsroom/newsroom_factsheet.htm, accessed October 13, 2002.

[28]NSTC is the cabinet-level council that provides the principal means for the president to coordinate science, space, and technology issues across the diverse parts of the federal research and development enterprise.

[29]See National Science and Technology Council (2002).

[30]National Science and Technology Council (1995a).

In December 1994, a large workshop of industry and government leaders gathered at the White House to establish priorities among the respective industry segments and to develop research agendas and action plans for achieving their highest-priority goals. Among those representing residential construction were homebuilders, product manufacturers, code officials, and insurers.

The efforts that led to the development, endorsement, and initial implementation of the National Construction Goals involved significant cooperation between the public and private sectors. This cooperation also provided a more inclusive process that helped ensure that the efforts had the support of the entire industry. As a result, this effort gave rise to other efforts including the Partnership for the Advancement of Infrastructure and its Renewal (PAIR)—an effort to streamline the nation's building regulatory system—and the development of an implementation plan for the residential sector's portion of the National Construction Goals. This plan was prepared with significant input throughout the residential construction industry and it placed the highest priority on two goals:[31]

- reducing production cost through improved technology, and

- improving product durability.

The plan identified several strategies for achieving these goals including improving the efficiency of the housing production process; establishing and maintaining an information infrastructure that responds to the needs of builders, subcontractors, designers, manufacturers, code officials, and consumers; and fostering the development and commercialization of products and systems using input from the building community.

Building America. Launched in 1996, DOE's Building America program is a voluntary public-private partnership that provides energy solutions in housing production.[32] Building America uses a systems engineering approach to home building to

---

[31] NAHB Research Center (1998).

[32] O'Brien et al. (2000); and "Building America" at www.buildingamerica.gov.

- produce homes on a community scale that use 30 percent to 50 percent less energy,

- help builders reduce construction time and waste by as much as 50 percent,

- improve builder productivity,

- provide new product opportunities to manufacturers and suppliers, and

- implement innovative energy- and material-saving technologies.

To accomplish these goals, Building America performs research, development, and testing; education and technical assistance; and analyses of factory and site construction processes. The centerpiece of these efforts are its five Building America teams. Comprising more than 50 companies and organizations, these teams unite segments of the building industry that traditionally work independently of one another.[33]

Throughout the design and construction process, these teams use systems engineering to consider the interactions among the building site, envelope, and mechanical systems. This improves the understanding of how one component in a house can greatly affect others. This then allows the teams to incorporate energy-saving strategies into these homes at no extra cost. (Reinvesting these cost savings in improved energy performance and product quality is a Building America requirement.)

Partnership for Advancing Technology in Housing. Based on the National Construction Goals and the residential implementation plan, PATH was launched in 1998. It was created through the cooperative efforts of the Subcommittee on Construction and Building, the White House Office of Science and Technology Policy, HUD, DOE, and others as a public-private partnership involving homebuilders, federal agencies, product innovators, researchers, industry professionals and housing institutions, developers, and nonprofits. As a voluntary initiative, it seeks to foster partnerships among indus-

---

[33]U.S. Department of Energy (2002c).

try, government, and education institutions to facilitate the advancement and adoption of new and existing technologies.

Managed by HUD, PATH has three goals: (1) research and development, (2) information and outreach, and (3) planning and barriers analysis. PATH pursues these goals through a variety of activities aimed at linking technology forecasting and R&D with steps necessary to introduce innovations to the market and encourage their acceptance. Examples of PATH efforts to achieve these goals follow:

- To advance research and development of housing technologies, PATH works with a number of federal partners. Examples include leveraging PATH funds and National Science Foundation funds to conduct basic research on housing-related technologies; working with the Forest Products Laboratory of the Department of Agriculture to develop reliability-based design for housing in high wind areas; and helping the National Institute of Standards and Technology develop methods to evaluate housing technology.

- To increase information flow and outreach, PATH works with a variety of public, private, and nonprofit organizations to develop regulatory assistance programs to support new technology deployment, create an inventory of innovative technology, conduct technology evaluations and demonstrations, and disseminate information about housing technologies to industry and public audiences. PATH also cooperates with other agencies such as the Department of Energy to promote and improve awareness of pilot projects and field trials.

- To improve planning and barrier analysis, PATH sponsors technology roadmaps[34] to help set the strategic R&D planning process for PATH and the industry as a whole. Roadmapping efforts to date have examined the use of information technology to streamline the homebuilding process; the application of advanced, panelized-type systems to housing construction; whole

---

[34]DOE's Office of Building, Technology, State and Community Programs has also conducted numerous technology roadmaps on such diverse areas as windows, lighting, the building envelope, and commercial buildings. These roadmaps were developed with significant and diverse involvement by government and industry. For more information, see www.eren.doe.gov/buildings/technology_roadmaps/.

house and building process design; and energy efficiency in existing buildings. PATH also funds technology reviews to better understand why some innovations succeed while others do not, as well as policy and market research to identify economic, regulatory, and institutional barriers to housing technology and innovation. This RAND study on innovation in the housing industry is one such effort.[35]

SUMMARY

Although this chapter has not reviewed all past federal efforts, it provides a sense of the evolution in goals, scope, and strategies used during the last 40 years. Perhaps the most important finding from this chapter is that the government has repeatedly recognized the benefits of innovation and the challenges that confront innovation in the housing industry. For this reason, the federal government has repeatedly invested in efforts to increase the rate of innovation in housing.

The next major finding is that the federal government has sought to learn from past experiences and to develop new strategies to better address the innovation process. In reviewing these past efforts, three major changes in the federal approach to promoting innovation in housing are evident.

The first is the move from a top-down to bottom-up approach. Earlier government programs frequently designated particular types of technology and directed industry to apply them. There was little consultation with stakeholders inside or outside of the industry or even across government departments and agencies. Today, instead of picking specific technologies and innovations, government programs generally seek to stimulate private and public efforts to develop technologies and innovations.

The second major change is the broadening interpretation of technology and innovation and how they are applied to housing. In the 1960s and early 1970s, technology and innovation largely meant the direct application of engineering advances to improve specific as-

---

[35]See the PATH web site at www.pathnet.org.

pects of housing production, such as industrializing home manufacturing processes. By the 1990s, thinking about technology and innovation expanded to include the application of information technology to integrate various housing production processes.

Third, perspectives on how to promote innovation in housing have increasingly focused on broader whole-house and systems approaches that integrate many aspects of the homebuilding process over narrower and more targeted efforts.

As a result of these changes, federal efforts to promote innovation in housing have evolved for the better. Even though federal approaches have become more effective, it is important to ask whether federal efforts to promote innovation in housing can be further improved. Chapter Six, the last of this report, presents a range of strategies that could improve the innovation process in the housing industry.

Chapter Six

FEDERAL STRATEGIES FOR PROMOTING INNOVATION IN HOUSING

Over the past 100 years, significant innovations have occurred in the housing industry. Despite these accomplishments, industry characteristics and participant motives can present challenges to the innovation process that likely reduce and slow the industry's rate of innovation.

This report has shown that the federal government has long recognized both the benefits and challenges associated with innovation and has invested in R&D, passed laws to facilitate technology transfer, and created federal programs to support and accelerate innovation in this industry.

It is precisely because the benefits of innovation are so great and because the need for innovation continues today that this report proposes strategies to improve innovation within the existing industry rather than calling for reforms that will be difficult or impractical to implement.

STRUCTURING STRATEGIES TO IMPROVE INNOVATION

This report closes by proposing strategies that the federal government can use to improve innovation. These strategies are organized according to the innovation model presented in Chapter Two. Shown below, this model can be thought of as having four primary components as labeled on the right of Figure 6.1: research, knowledge base, the ID3 pipeline, and market forces.

RAND*MR1658-6.1*

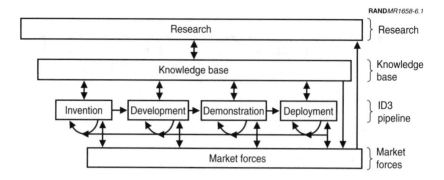

Figure 6.1—Key Components of the Housing Innovation Process

Since each component of the innovation process has unique needs and difficulties, this report proposes four sets of matching strategies:

• enhance research activities,

• strengthen the knowledge base,

• support the ID3 pipeline, and

• improve market linkages.

In the following sections, these strategies are presented and we explain how each could potentially strengthen the corresponding component of the innovation process. In most cases, the strategies are similar to existing government policies, programs, or investments, although they may be new to housing or used in a different capacity than at present.

In general, these strategies focus on adding support to missing or poorly functioning aspects of the housing innovation process. By helping to build the missing infrastructure, these efforts can help increase the rate of innovation and the resulting benefits.

These strategies are not listed by hierarchy, order of importance, or priority for implementation. Furthermore, they are not likely to be equally effective or cost-effective. That said, these strategies and, more generally, this report's systematic discussion of innovation should help the housing industry's many participants candidly and constructively consider ways to increase innovation within the existing structure and characteristics of the industry.

ENHANCE RESEARCH ACTIVITIES

Sustained Research Support

Federal government agencies should continue to support research, especially basic and exploratory research, because such research is generally high risk, expensive, and difficult to appropriate the benefits from. Furthermore, given that the housing industry, especially its many small and medium-sized firms, has limited funds available for investing in R&D, the portion available for basic research is exceptionally small. Therefore, the federal government has a critical role in investing in basic research to expand the knowledge base that underlies the entire innovation process.

STRENGTHEN THE KNOWLEDGE BASE

Support Networking Across Horizontal and Vertical Boundaries

Network building has long been recognized as critical to innovation. A recent affirmation of networks and the government's role in promoting them can be found in a 1998 report by the Committee on Science of the U.S. House of Representatives (1998):

> One of the strengths of the U.S. research and development system has been its ability to harness various sources of innovation in U.S. society—the private sector, universities, and public laboratories. The U.S. government has helped to bring this about by adopting policies and programs designed to encourage networking among the various sectors.

Given the importance of such networks, the federal government could expand network building across the horizontal and vertical fragmentation that characterizes the industry. Conferences, symposia, roadmapping, and other collaborative events can be designed to provide opportunities for close interaction between the practitioners of homebuilding and the scientists and engineers who work in the research divisions of various sectors. These exchanges can help competitors, collaborators, suppliers, consumers, and regulators communicate, educate, and build bridges across disciplines and interests.[1] For example, the government can use its resources, technical capabilities, and influence to bring parties from upstream or downstream segments together to strengthen their connections.[2] Alternatively, the government can work with existing associations and state and local networks while also helping to create a longer-term, self-supporting network.

Coordinate Government Efforts

Government departments and agencies fund research and programs to pursue their individual missions and goals. In doing so, they inevitably duplicate the funding of some research while unintentionally neglecting others. Although competing efforts can sometimes be desirable, they may also illustrate where better coordination within and across government agencies could help bridge knowledge gaps, minimize waste and redundancies, and maximize the leveraging of resources.

The need for increased coordination is not limited solely to the federal government. Many state governments have created science and technology promotion offices since the mid-1980s, and an increasing number of states have a science and technology component in their economic development plans. In fact, by 1995, state governments collectively spent more than $3 billion on R&D activities, with about 80 percent funding research at state universities.[3] As a result, improving federal coordination with state and local governments including code officials could accelerate the diffusion and adoption of innovations. Finally, coordination with local government could also be beneficial because building codes, zoning regulations, and insurance rates are regulated at the state and local levels. If coordination could draw these participants into the innovation process (and into the innovation decisionmaking process) earlier, an innovation could have a better chance of being successfully deployed.

---

[1]In some cases, participating firms must be careful to avoid antitrust violations.

[2]Popper et al. (1998).

[3]Jankowski (1999).

Search and Disseminate Information on Relevant Federal R&D

In FY 1999, the federal government invested roughly $236 million in more than 500 housing-related R&D projects. Although some participants in the housing industry can dedicate time to learn about some or perhaps even all of these projects, most cannot. Efforts to increase awareness of this body of research and to make gaining such awareness easier can be particularly valuable. However, even efforts focused solely on housing will miss the potential for spillover technologies from other parts of the construction R&D portfolio, or even from areas further removed. A recent publication and spreadsheet[4] can aid these efforts. The RaDiUS database,[5] in particular, can help one search the entire federal R&D portfolio. However, varying degrees of time and effort are still required to obtain, search, and find information of interest.

To facilitate this discovery and sharing of knowledge among those in the larger housing community, governments could consider regularly preparing and disseminating pre-searched and pre-sorted information while making tools (such as RaDiUS) more widely known and accessible. This could also ensure that the results of government-funded research are adequately documented so that the key aspects of the project can be found quickly and shared with others.

Support Education and Training

Education and training are critical to the creation, adoption, and diffusion of innovations. A workforce that is literate and able to think, analyze, and apply new solutions to problems can more effectively create and adopt innovations. Such a workforce might also be better empowered to benefit from and accept innovations.

One may argue that industry should fund the education and training of its workers, but a government role—although not necessarily a federal government role—might be necessitated by two characteris-

---

[4]Hassell et al. (2001). The report and the corresponding Excel spreadsheet can be downloaded from www.pathnet.org/resource/radius.html.

[5]For more information on RaDiUS, see www.rand.org/radius.

tics of the industry. First, most homebuilders are small and lack the resources to invest in improving the skills of their workers. Second, employment is highly mobile and subcontracting is prominent. For these reasons, homebuilders have few incentives to invest in improving the skills of workers who may or may not work with them again in the future and whose knowledge and skills could soon benefit a competitor.

Hence, one or more levels of government may want to support such efforts (either through direct expenditures or through tax incentives), at least when there is a clear public benefit to such training.

SUPPORT THE ID3 PIPELINE

In addition to supporting research and the sharing of knowledge, the federal government should consider strengthening the core steps of the technology development process, namely, invention, development, demonstration, and deployment also known as the ID3 pipeline. Relevant strategies include improving technology transfer, increasing incentives to perform R&D, and supporting development, demonstration, and deployment.

Support Exploratory and Applied Research for Technology Transfer

Beyond identifying and disseminating information on completed R&D projects, the federal government could also increase support for exploratory and applied research on how existing technologies could be transferred to housing applications. At present, there is only limited support for these activities. A government-wide initiative could bring together participants from industry, government, and academia to identify technologies in the federal R&D portfolio and to transfer them to the housing industry.

An additional strategy for expanding technology transfer would be to create or expand housing-related innovation programs similar to the Small Business Innovation Research (SBIR) programs. At present, federal agencies that receive over $100 million annually for external R&D are required to have SBIR programs to fund exploratory and applied research for technology transfer. Expanding these programs where they exist or creating them where they do not could help promote innovation within the largest component of the homebuilding industry.[6]

Modify the Research and Experiment Tax Credit for Small Firms

As currently formulated, the research and experiment tax credit provides a tax incentive for firms to increase their R&D investments. However, this incentive applies only to R&D that is conducted beyond a base amount. For this reason, this tax credit is more effective at expanding R&D programs at large firms than at helping to establish them at small firms. Reviewing the structure of this tax credit could determine if it could better address the needs of small firms, thereby providing another boost to the ID3 pipeline.

Support Development and Demonstration

Beyond research, technology transfer, and invention come development and demonstration. Unfortunately, both of these activities are costly and high risk and offer no guarantee of commercial success. As a result, funding such activities can be difficult, especially for (1) high-risk innovations, (2) small firms, and (3) innovations that produce public benefits but limited benefits to industry participants.

For these reasons, the government could create cooperative efforts between firms and government laboratories, enable the formation of industrial consortia to share costs, or even provide cost-shared support. Such efforts would help good ideas move beyond invention and early-stage development. They could highlight the existence of an innovation, demonstrate the soundness of a technology, provide opportunities to evaluate performance, and stimulate industry interest in commercial production. Finally, these efforts could provide information to help inform decisions about compliance with codes and standards.

---

[6]Although HUD does not have an SBIR program, the agency is very active in supporting small businesses through its regular procedures. In addition, within HUD, PATH Technology Development Grants are available to, but not dedicated to, small businesses.

Explain the Regulatory Process to Innovators

For an innovation to be accepted by the regulatory system, at a minimum it must be tested, certified, and evaluated. Once an evaluation report is prepared, these early steps may seem easy relative to educating code officials throughout the country about the product. Similarly, changing the model code (and ultimately state and local codes) so that it explicitly allows an innovation can be an even more difficult task. Although each of these steps can be expensive individually, they become more so the longer they are put off because of lack of understanding or bad planning. The government could improve the ID3 process by helping to communicate the importance of these issues to innovators early on (or even providing technical assistance) so that they better understand how the process works.

Provide Technical and Standard Development Support

The government could also expand its efforts to provide technical support to the housing industry, especially by working to link the human and physical assets of the national laboratories and their manufacturing extension programs with the needs and interests of housing innovators.

In addition, innovations are often not accepted until their benefits can be measured and reliably demonstrated. Developing standards to measure performance and reliability is another area where the government could play an important role.

Public Procurement

In those cases where the government is a potential customer for an innovation, it should consider directly purchasing the innovation. The need to spend taxpayer dollars responsibly dictates that prices be reasonable, but large and sustained purchases by the government can help lower the cost because of the lower risk and long-term commitment. Although government regulations currently require awarding purchases to the lowest bid, the government could consider giving preferential treatment to the use of innovative materials, products, or services. For example, during the construction or rehabilitation of public and military housing, the government could require that light fixtures meet certain energy-efficiency standards. Similarly, federally supported public housing authorities or the federal Weatherization Assistance Program could provide the government with an opportunity to use its purchasing power.

IMPROVE MARKET LINKAGES

Finally, the government can also help promote innovation by improving the linkages among market forces and all other components of the innovation process. Candidate strategies include collecting and analyzing data on market trends, monitoring the performance of innovations, creating linkages among currently independent markets, and creating incentives for end users.

Help Identify Market Trends and Opportunities

The federal government could expand its efforts to identify, analyze, and increase awareness of market trends and opportunities. This is especially true when the rate of innovation is slowed by information barriers, market failures, and externalities. Through credible data collection, analysis, and dissemination, the government could increase awareness of market trends and the opportunities for innovation and ultimately help the private sector focus on finding innovative solutions to public problems. Although federally supported efforts may overlap those of the private sector, government efforts could focus on opportunities related to correcting externalities and increasing the provision of public benefits.

Support Product Performance Monitoring and Evaluation

The federal government could also help monitor and evaluate the performance and adoption of innovations. As noted in Chapter Four, many industry participants stress the need for more reliable information to help assess the potential applications, costs, and benefits of innovations.

Reward Important Innovations with Valuable Recognition

The federal government could also recognize firms and individuals responsible for important housing innovations. Although not federally sponsored, current examples include the Innovative Housing Technology Awards jointly awarded by *Popular Science* magazine and the NAHB Research Center.[7] A similar though different approach is that of EnergyStar, which allows highly energy-efficient products to use the EnergyStar label to increase the recognition of their products.

However, these existing awards may not target areas most in need of technological change. New recognitions and awards could target areas needing improvement such as water conservation, peak load management, or regulatory streamlining. The federal government might also work in partnership with state and local governments, research institutions, professional and industry associations, and nonprofit organizations both to identify technology needs and to evaluate innovations worthy of recognition.

If implemented, such awards might accelerate innovation for several reasons. First, recognition and awards, as marks of excellence, might increase the visibility and credibility of innovations and their innovators and help innovators to secure additional funding for further R&D, commercialize production, or boost sales. Second, they might increase a firm's focus on R&D investment and encourage further improvement. Third, awards might increase confidence in an innovation and people's willingness to adopt it. Fourth, they might send a signal to regulators, industry associations, producers, and retailers, prompting them to examine the innovation and find ways to expand its application or share in the market.

Create Linkages Among Markets

Next, the federal government can play a role in creating linkages among markets that are currently independent. Today's economy is characterized by many different markets for capital, commodities, and managing risk. Linking these markets and allowing them to in-

---

[7]Phillips (2001, p. 72).

teract easily and at low cost not only provides profitmaking opportunities, but it also helps increase technical and economic efficiency. However, this is only possible once the institutional infrastructure is in place to link markets and the transaction costs are low enough to justify the extra effort. Although improved economic efficiency can sometimes be a sufficient justification for federal involvement, cases where linking markets can reduce externalities and increase public benefits are particularly appropriate for federal involvement. In so doing, externalities can be internalized and market forces can lead to more efficient outcomes.

Examples of creating linkages among independent markets include the following:

- Link residential investments in energy efficiency and renewable energy to the market for traditional air emissions permits (e.g., sulfur dioxide and nitrogen oxides) as well as the small but growing international market for greenhouse gas "emission reduction credits."[8]

- Securitize the value of emissions permits or reductions for the life of a mortgage so that the reductions can help finance investments in energy efficiency of renewable energy sources; this could benefit the homeowner, the builder, or a third party.

- Rigorously measure and demonstrate that innovations can reduce the risk of natural hazards and use that information to change how insurers approach innovations for which there are no actuarial data; this would help increase the demand for innovations that reduce insurance costs.

Create Financial Incentives for End Users

Finally, to help new markets grow, the government could consider subsidizing the use of innovations, particularly if the innovation

---

[8]The United States does not currently have a domestic program to manage greenhouse gas emissions, but there is an active if currently small market for greenhouse gas emission reduction credits. The principal market participants are firms seeking to hedge their risks against long-term regulation or those seeking to be even partly compensated for reducing emissions today. For more information, see the Greenhouse Gas Brokerage of Natsource's web site at www.natsource.com.

could reduce an externality or increase the provision of public benefits. Whether the subsidy is direct or indirect (e.g., a tax credit), it would help increase the use of an innovation. The government might give a higher tax credit to homeowners who use innovations that have a small foothold in the market or those that support priorities in the National Construction Goals, just as it does with the wind production tax credit and the alternative fuel vehicle tax credits.

Furthermore, state and local subsidies could be combined with federal subsidies. This is especially relevant if using an innovation could provide state- or local-level benefits such as reduced water consumption or reduced peak electrical load.

CONCLUSIONS

The strategies the federal government can use to promote innovation presented in this report were based on a systematic examination of what could improve innovation in housing. As a result, this report has suggested how each strategy can supply the infrastructure needed to more fully support the research, knowledge, technology development, and market forces needed for successful innovation. Although each of these strategies is potentially beneficial, for several reasons the strategies should be viewed as a menu of options available to the federal government:

- These strategies are representative, not exhaustive. As a result, other instruments may be more effective or appropriate.

- Even though each strategy can potentially play an important part in creating a better functioning innovation process, not all strategies may be needed.

- This report has neither analyzed nor speculated on the cost-effectiveness of individual strategies and, as a result, cannot suggest the optimal combination of these strategies.

Thus, although this menu cannot tell decisionmakers what to do, it does provide a useful structure for citizens, industry participants, and government officials to discuss innovation, learn from past efforts, and consider new efforts that can work within the existing industry rather than seek to change the industry.

For example, this report can be used as a conceptual framework for federal, state, and local policymakers to consider how different agencies and levels of government can cooperate, coordinate, and leverage their activities to better support the innovation process. It can also be used by public-private partnerships to help each sector better understand and complement the other. Finally, it can also be used to improve existing programs or to create new programs or policies to fill holes and complement other programs.

In closing, it is important to realize that using this framework alone will not ensure a better functioning innovation process. The programs themselves must also prepare and execute solid management plans that specify goals, measure performance, and adjust strategies as conditions change and the effectiveness and cost-effectiveness of each becomes apparent.[9] Thus, this report does not independently provide the answer to how to increase the rate of innovation in housing, but it does show how a better understanding of the innovation process and the housing industry can be used to improve the ways in which innovation occurs in the housing industry.

-----

[9]See the large and growing body of work on the Government Performance and Results Act, including those by the U.S. General Accounting Office.

BIBLIOGRAPHY

Anderson, Beverly J., "Technology Strategy for the Construction Industry," in C. William Ibbs, ed., *Construction Congress: Proceedings of the 1995 Conference*, New York: American Society of Civil Engineers Press, 1995, pp. 9–16.

Arthur D. Little, Inc., *Patterns and Problems of Technical Innovation in American Industry*, Cambridge, Mass.: Arthur D. Little, Inc., C-65344, September 1963.

Baer, Walter, C. Johnston Conover, Cheryl Cook, Patricia Fleischauer, Bruce Goeller, William Herdman, Leland Johnson, Edward Merrow, Richard Rettig, and John Wirt, *An Analysis of Federally Funded Demonstration Projects: Supporting Case Studies*, Santa Monica, Calif.: RAND, R-1927-DOC, 1976, pp. L1–L97.

Barta, Patrick, "Why Big Lenders Are So Afraid of Fannie Mae and Freddie Mac," *The Wall Street Journal*, April 5, 2001.

Bauman, Richard D., and Joseph J. Kracum, "Innovation—What More Can We Do?" in C. William Ibbs, ed., *Construction Congress: Proceedings of the 1995 Conference*, New York: American Society of Civil Engineers Press, 1995, pp. 65–69.

Bernstein, Harvey M., and Andrew C. Lemer, *Solving the Innovation Puzzle: Challenges Facing the U.S. Design and Construction Industry*, New York: American Society of Civil Engineers, 1996.

Bijker, Wiebe E., Thomas P. Hughes, and Trevor Pinch, *The Social Construction of Technological Systems*, Cambridge, Mass.: The MIT Press, 1987.

Bijker, Wiebe E., and John Law, eds., *Shaping Technology/Building Society: Studies in Sociotechnical Change*, Cambridge, Mass.: The MIT Press, 2000.

Blackley, Dixie M., and Edward M. Shepard, III, "The Diffusion of Innovation in Home Building," *Journal of Housing Economics*, Vol. 5, 1996, pp. 303–322.

Blanpied, William A., ed., *Impacts of the Early Cold War on the Formulation of U.S. Science Policy: Selected Memoranda of William T. Golden, October 1950–April 1951*, Washington, D.C.: American Association for the Advancement of Science, 2000.

Chapman, Robert E., *An Approach for Measuring Reductions in Construction Worker Illnesses and Injuries: Baseline Measures of Construction Industry Practices for the National Construction Goals*, Gaithersburg, Md.: National Institute of Standards and Technology, NISTIR 6473, September 2000.

Civil Engineering Research Foundation, *National Construction Goals: A Construction Industry Perspective*, Washington, D.C., circa 1995a.

_____, *National Construction Sector Goals: Industry Strategies for Implementation*, Washington, D.C.: National Institute of Standards and Technology, NIST-GCR-95-680, July 1995b.

_____, "Priorities for Federal Innovation Reform: Reforming Federal Policy in Order to Enhance Innovation within the Design and Construction Industry: Federal Policies in Support of a National Innovation System," Washington, D.C., n.d.

Council of Economic Advisors, *Economic Report of the President*, Washington, D.C.: U.S. Government Printing Office, 2000.

Dietz, Albert G. H., "Housing Industry Research," in Burnham Kelly, Castle N. Day, Albert G. H. Dietz, John T. Dunlop, Carl Koch, James A. Murray, Hideo Sasaki, and Bernard P. Spring, eds., *Design and the Production of Houses*," New York: McGraw-Hill Book Company, Inc., 1959.

Dowall, David E., and Lawrence C. Barone, "Improving Construction Industry Performance: Issues and Opportunities," Berkeley, Calif.:

Center for Real Estate and Urban Economics, working paper No. 94-220, University of California, Berkeley, September 1993.

Energy Information Administration, "Changes in Energy Usage in Residential Housing Units," available at www.eia.doe.gov/emeu/rrecs/recs97/decade.html, accessed March 25, 2002.

Enterprise Foundation, "How We Help: Affordable Homes," available at www.enterprisefoundation.org/about/whatwedo/affordablehousing.asp, July 15, 2002.

Fannie Mae, "Housing and Environment Initiative," available at www.efanniemaecom/hcd/single_family/mortgage_products/environment.html, accessed March 28, 2002.

Farhar, Barbara, *Pilot States Program Report: Home Energy Rating Systems and Energy-Efficient Mortgages*, Golden, Colo.: National Energy Renewal Laboratory, NREL/TP-550-27722, April 2000.

Federal Trade Commission, "Energy Labels: After 20 Years, Still a Bright Idea," available at www.ftc.gov/bcp/conline/edcams/appliances/20years.htm, accessed April 26, 2002.

Field, Charles G., and Steven R. Rivkin, *The Building Code Burden*, Lexington, Mass.: Lexington Books, 1975.

Freddie Mac, *Automated Underwriting: Making Mortgage Lending Simpler and Fairer for America's Families*, McLean, Va., September 1996, available at www.freddiemac.com/homeownership/au-works, accessed July 15, 2002.

Gerwick, Ben C., Jr., "Implementing Construction Research," *Journal of Construction Engineering and Management*, Vol. 116, No. 4, December 1990, pp. 556–563.

Hansen, Karen Lee, and C. B. Tatum, "Technology and Strategic Management in Construction," *Journal of Management in Engineering,"* Vol. 5, No. 1, January 1989.

Harney, Kenneth, "Online Storehouse of Appraisal Data to Aid Buyers," *The Washington Post*, June 24, 2000, p. G01.

Hassell, Scott, Mark Bernstein, and Aimee Bower, *The Role of Information Technology in Housing Design and Construction*, Santa Monica, Calif.: RAND, CF-156-OSTP, 2000.

Hassell, Scott, Scott Florence, and Emile Ettedgui, *Summary of Federal Construction, Building and Housing-Related Research and Development in FY1999*, Santa Monica, Calif.: RAND, MR-1390-HUD/NIST, 2001.

Holman Enterprises Ltd., *Innovation in the Housing Industry*, Ottawa, Ontario: National Research Council of Canada, Institute for Research in Construction, December 2001.

Ibbs, C. William, ed., *Construction Congress: Proceedings of the 1995 Conference*, New York: American Society of Civil Engineers Press, 1995.

Jankowski, John W., *What Is the State Government Role in the R&D Enterprise?* Arlington, Va.: National Science Foundation, NSF 99-348, 1999.

Johnston, David W., and Daren E. Marceau, "Forces Affecting Construction Technology Research and Development," in C. William Ibbs, ed., *Construction Congress: Proceedings of the 1995 Conference*, New York: American Society of Civil Engineers Press, 1995, pp. 33–40.

Joint Center for Housing Studies of Harvard University, *The State of the Nation's Housing 2002*, Cambridge, Mass., 2002.

Keoleian, Gregory A., Steven Blanchard, and Peter Reppe, "Life-Cycle Energy, Costs, and Strategies for Improving a Single-Family House," *Journal of Industrial Ecology*, Vol. 4, No. 2, 2000, pp. 135–156.

Kirkman, David C., and Enrique K. Muller, *Design and Development of Housing Systems for Operation Breakthrough Phase I*, Seattle, Wash.: Boeing Aerospace Co., 1973.

Kline, Stephen, and Nathan Rosenberg, "An Overview of Innovation," in Ralph Landau and Nathan Rosenberg, eds., *Positive Sum Strategy: Harnessing Technology for Economic Growth*, Washington, D.C.: National Academy Press, 1986, pp. 275–306.

Koebel, C. Theodore, Maria Papadakis, and Elizabeth Matthews, "The Diffusion of Innovation Literature as It Applies to the Residential Building Industry," draft, Blacksburg, Va.: Center for Housing Research, Virginia Polytechnic Institute and State University, January 2002.

LaCour-Little, Michael, "The Evolving Role of Technology in Mortgage Finance," *Journal of Housing Research*, Vol. 11, No. 2, 2000, pp. 173–205.

Larson, Charles, "R&D and Innovation in Industry," available at www.iriinc.org/web/Publications/aaas.cfm, accessed January 11, 2002.

Lutz, James D., and Ossama M. Salem, "Strategies for Fostering Enabling Technologies," in C. William Ibbs, ed., *Construction Congress: Proceedings of the 1995 Conference*, New York: American Society of Civil Engineers Press, 1995, pp. 573–579.

Manseau, Andre, and George Seaden, eds., *Innovation in Construction: An International Review of Public Policies*, London: Spon Press, 2001.

Mitropoulos, Panagiotis, and C. B. Tatum, "Process and Criteria for Technology Adoption Decisions," in C. William Ibbs, ed., *Construction Congress: Proceedings of the 1995 Conference*, New York: American Society of Civil Engineers Press, 1995, pp. 17–24.

Mowery, David C., and Nathan Rosenberg, "The Influence of Market Demand Upon Innovation: A Critical Review of Some Recent Empirical Studies," in Nathan Rosenberg, ed., *Inside the Black Box: Technology and Economics*, Cambridge, England: Cambridge University Press, 1982, pp. 193–241.

NAHB Research Center, *Historical Review of Housing Innovations*, Upper Marlboro, Md., October 1989a.

_____, *Criteria for Evaluation of Emerging Housing Technologies*, Upper Marlboro, Md., November 1989b.

_____, *Advanced Housing Technology Program: Phase I*, Upper Marlboro, Md., September 27, 1991.

_____, *Cycle-Time Reduction in the Residential Construction Process*, Upper Marlboro, Md., June 4, 1993.

_____, *Domestic and International Housing Technology Research*, Upper Marlboro, Md., April 15, 1994.

_____, *Building Better Homes at Lower Costs: The Industry Implementation Plan for the Residential National Construction Goals*, Upper Marlboro, Md., January 13, 1998.

_____, "Advanced Panelized Construction Roadmap," draft, Upper Marlboro, Md., 2001a.

_____, "PATH Roadmap for Information Technology to Accelerate and Streamline Home Building," draft, Upper Marlboro, Md., April 2001b.

_____, *Commercialization of Innovations: Lessons Learned*, Upper Marlboro, Md., August 28, 2001c.

_____, *Housing Innovation and the Appraisal Process*, Upper Marlboro, Md., August 5, 2002.

NAHB Research Center, Burton Goldberg, and Edward Shepard, *Diffusion of Innovation in the Housing Industry*, Upper Marlboro, Md., November 1989.

Nam, C. H., and C. B. Tatum, "Toward Understanding of Product Innovation Process in Construction," *Journal of Construction Engineering and Management*, Vol. 115, No. 4, December 1989, pp. 517–534.

_____, "Strategies for Technology Push: Lessons from Construction Innovations," *Journal of Construction Engineering and Management*, Vol. 118, No. 3, September 1992, pp. 507–524.

National Evaluation Service, *Developing and Deploying New Building Technologies Through Technology Acceptance Planning*, Falls Church, Va., forthcoming.

National Institute of Building Science, "Workshop on National Construction Goals as Related to the Commercial and Institutional Building Sector," draft, Washington, D.C., September 18, 1996.

National Research Council, Board on Infrastructure and the Constructed Environment, Committee for Oversight and Assessment of the Partnership for Advancing Technology in Housing, *The Partnership for Advancing Technology in Housing: Year 2000 Progress Assessment of the PATH Program*, Washington, D.C.: National Academy Press, 2000.

National Research Council, Board on Energy and Environmental Systems, Committee on Benefits of DOE R&D on Energy Efficiency and Fossil Energy, *Energy Research at DOE: Was It Worth It? Energy Efficiency and Fossil Energy Research 1978 to 2000*, Washington, D.C.: National Academy Press, 2001.

National Science Board, "Government Funding of Scientific Research," working paper, NSB-97-186, available at www.nsf.gov/nsb/documents/1997/nsb97186/nsb97186.htm, November 20, 2001.

National Science and Technology Council, Committee on Civilian Industrial Technology, Subcommittee on Construction and Building, *Program of the Subcommittee on Construction and Building*, Gaithersburg, Md.: National Institute of Standards and Technology, NISTIR 5443-A, July 1994a.

_____, *Rationale and Preliminary Plan for Federal Research for Construction and Building*, Gaithersburg, Md.: National Institute of Standards and Technology, NISTIR 5536, November 1994b.

_____, *Construction and Building: Federal Research and Development in Support of the U.S. Construction Industry*, Washington, D.C., 1995a.

_____, *National Planning for Construction and Building R&D*, Gaithersburg, Md.: National Institute of Standards and Technology, NISTIR 5759, December 1995b.

_____, Committee on Technology, Subcommittee on Construction and Building, *Construction and Building: Interagency Program for Technical Advancement in Construction and Building*, Washington, D.C., 1999.

_____, Subcommittee on Construction and Building, available at www.bfrl.nist.gov/860/c_b/, accessed July 15, 2002.

North Carolina Solar Center, fact sheet, "Selecting a Site" available at www.ncsc.ncsu.edu/fact/07body.htm, accessed June 8, 2002.

O'Brien, Michael, Ron Wakefield, and Yvan Beliveau, *Industrializing the Residential Construction Site: Phase I*, Blacksburg, Va.: Center for Housing Research, Virginia Polytechnic Institute and State University, July 2000.

Ortiz, David Santana, and Mark Allen Bernstein, *Measures of Residential Energy Consumption and Their Relationship to DOE Policy*, Santa Monica, Calif.: RAND, MR-1105-DOE, 1999.

PATH Working Group on Barriers/Insurance, "A Partnership for Advancing Technology in Housing Position Paper: Homeowner's Insurance as a Tool for the Adoption of Innovation," draft, Washington, D.C., November 24, 1999.

_____, "A Partnership for Advancing Technology in Housing Position Paper: Liability Insurance for the Homebuilding Industry," draft, Washington, D.C., September 1, 2000.

Phillips, William, "2001 Innovative Housing Technology Awards," *Popular Science*, March 2001, pp. 72–74.

Popper, Steven W., Caroline S. Wagner, and Eric V. Larson, *New Forces at Work: Industry Views Critical Technologies*, Santa Monica, Calif.: RAND, MR-1008-1-OSTP, 1998.

President's Committee of Advisors on Science and Technology (PCAST), Panel on Energy Research and Development, *Report to the President on Federal Energy Research and Development for the Challenges of the Twenty-First Century*, Washington, D.C.: Executive Office of the President, November 1997.

_____, Panel on International Cooperation in Energy Research, Development, Demonstration, and Deployment, *Powerful Partnerships: The Federal Role in International Cooperation on Energy Innovation*, Washington, D.C.: Executive Office of the President, June 1999.

Rohe, William M., George McCarthy, and Shannon Van Zandt, "The Social Benefits and Costs of Homeownership: A Critical Assessment of the Research," Washington, D.C.: Research Institute for

Housing America, working paper No. 00-01, May 2000, available at www.housingamerica.org/.

Rosefielde, Steven, and Daniel Quinn Mills, "Is Construction Technologically Stagnant?" in Julian E. Laupe and Daniel Quinn Mills, eds., *The Construction Industry*, Lexington, Mass.: Lexington Books, 1979.

Rosenberg, Nathan, "The Direction of Technological Change: Inducement Mechanisms and Focusing Devices," *Perspectives on Technology*, Cambridge, Mass.: Cambridge University Press, 1976.

Ruttan, Vernon, *Technology, Growth, and Development: An Induced Innovation Perspective*, New York: Oxford University Press, 2001.

Rybczynski, Witold, *Home: A Short History of an Idea*, New York: Viking, 1986.

Schlesinger, Tom, and Mark Erlich, "Housing: The Industry Capitalism Didn't Forget," in Rachel Bratt, Chester Hartman, and Ann Meyerson, eds., *Critical Perspectives on Housing*, Philadelphia, Penn.: Temple University Press, 1986, pp. 139–164.

Slaughter, E. Sarah, "Builders as Sources of Construction Innovation," *Journal of Construction Engineering and Management*, Vol. 119, No. 3, September 1993, pp. 532–549.

Strassmann, W. Paul, "Assessing the Knowledge of Innovations in Neglected Sectors: The Case of Residential Construction," in Patrick Kelly and Melvin Kranzberg, eds., *Technical Innovation: A Critical Review of Current Knowledge*, San Francisco, Calif.: San Francisco Press, Inc., pp. 263–273.

Sweaney, Anne L., Stacy Brock, Jane Defenbaugh Meier, and Kelly Shannon Manley, *The Development of a Housing Innovations Consumer Survey*, Athens, Ga.: Housing and Demographics Research Center, University of Georgia, April 25, 2001.

Tatum, C. B., "Potential Mechanism for Construction Innovation," *Journal of Construction Engineering and Management*, Vol. 112, No. 2, June 1986, pp. 178–191.

_____, "Process of Innovation in Construction Firms," *Journal of Construction Engineering and Management*, Vol. 118, No. 4, December 1987, pp. 648–663.

U.S. Census Bureau, *Multifamily Housing Construction*, Washington, D.C., EC97C-2332A(RV), October 1999a.

_____, *Single-Family Housing Construction*, Washington, D.C., EC97C-2332A(RV), November 1999b.

_____, *Nonemployer Statistics*, Washington, D.C., EC97X-CS4, January 2001a.

_____, *Expenditures for Residential Improvements and Repairs*, Current Construction Reports, Washington, D.C., C50/01-Q3, March 2001b.

_____, *Housing Completions*, Current Construction Reports, Washington, D.C., C22/01-3, May 2001c.

_____, *Housing Vacancy Survey—Fourth Quarter 2001*, Table 5, "Homeownership Rates in the United States," available at www.census.gov/hhes/www/housing/hvs/g401tab5.html, accessed March 25, 2002a.

_____, *Manufactured Homes Survey*, "Placements of New Manufactured Homes by Region and Size of Home," available at www.census.gov/constr/www/mhsindex.html, accessed June 19, 2002b.

U.S. Congress, *Housing and Urban Development Act of 1970*, P.L. 91-609, 1970.

U.S. Department of Commerce, Bureau of Economic Analysis, *National Income and Product Accounts*, 2002, available at www.bea.doc.gov/bea/dn/nipaweb/.

U.S. Department of Commerce and U.S. Department of Housing and Urban Development, *American Housing Survey for the United States: 1999*, Washington, D.C.: U.S. Government Printing Office, H150/99, October 2000.

U.S. Department of Energy, Office of Transportation Technologies, Office of Advanced Automotive Technologies, "Energy Secretary

Abraham Launches FreedomCAR, Replaces PNGV," Release No. PR-02-001, January 9, 2002a.

_____, Office of Energy Efficiency and Renewable Energy, *Energy Efficiency and Renewable Energy Strategic Program Review*, Washington, D.C., March 2002b.

_____, Office of Building Technology, State, and Community Programs, "Building America: Who We Are," available at www.eren.doe.gov/building/building_america/whoweare.shtml, accessed April 26, 2002c.

_____, Reference Brief on "Community Solar Access," available at www.eren.doe.gov/consumerinfo/refbriefs/ja1.html, accessed June 8, 2002d.

_____, "Financing an Energy Efficient Home," fact sheet, available at www.eren.doe/gov/erec/factsheets/feehome.html, accessed July 15, 2002e.

_____, "Small Business Innovation Research (SBIR) and Small Business Technology Transfer (STTR) Programs," available at sbir.er.doe.gov/sbir/, July 15, 2002f.

U.S. Department of Housing and Urban Development, Office of Policy Development and Research, *Partnership for Advancing Technology in Housing (PATH): Strategy and Operating Plan*, Washington, D.C., September 15, 2000.

U.S. Department of Labor, Bureau of Labor Statistics, "Career Guide to Industries: Construction," available at www.bls.gov/oco/cg/cgs003.htm, July 15, 2002.

U.S. General Accounting Office, *Measuring Performance: Strengths and Limitations of Research Indicators*, Washington, D.C.: GAO/RCED-97-91, March 1997.

U.S. House of Representatives, Committee on Science, *Unlocking the Future: Toward a New National Science Policy*, Washington, D.C., September 24, 1998, available at www.house.gov/science/science_policy_report.htm, July 15, 2002.

Ventre, Francis T., "Innovation in Residential Construction," *Technology Review*, November 1979.

Virginia Department of Planning and Zoning, "Land Development System (LDSnet)," Fairfax County, Va., available at www.co.fairfax.va.us/ldsnet/, n.d.

von Hippel, Eric, *The Sources of Innovation*, New York: Oxford University Press, 1988.

Wakefield, Ron, Michael O'Brien, and Yvan Beliveau, *Industrializing the Residential Construction Site. Phase II: Information Mapping*, Blacksburg, Va.: Center for Housing Research, Virginia Polytechnic Institute and State University, June 2001.